SMART MEMORY

...Techniques to Improve Memory

Tanushree Podder

GW00602699

Publishers
Pustak Mahal®

J-3/16 , Daryaganj, New Delhi-110002
☎ 23276539, 23272783, 23272784 • *Fax:* 011-23260518
E-mail: info@pustakmahal.com • *Website:* www.pustakmahal.com

Sales Centre
- 10-B, Netaji Subhash Marg, Daryaganj, New Delhi-110002
  ☎ 23268292, 23268293, 23279900 • *Fax:* 011-23280567
  E-mail: rapidexdelhi@indiatimes.com
- Hind Pustak Bhawan
  6686, Khari Baoli, Delhi-110006
  ☎ 23944314, 23911979

Branches
Bengaluru: ☎ 080-22234025 • *Telefax:* 080-22240209
E-mail: pustak@airtelmail.in • pustak@sancharnet.in
Mumbai: ☎ 022-22010941, 022-22053387
E-mail: rapidex@bom5.vsnl.net.in
Patna: ☎ 0612-3294193 • *Telefax:* 0612-2302719
E-mail: rapidexptn@rediffmail.com
Hyderabad: *Telefax:* 040-24737290
E-mail: pustakmahalhyd@yahoo.co.in

© **Pustak Mahal, New Delhi**

ISBN 978-81-223-0759-7

Edition: 2010

Printed at : Param Offsetters, Okhla, New Delhi-110020

Dedication

This book is dedicated to my father
who can still recite the poem
he learnt at the age of seven;
he is almost eighty.
I would love to be able to do
so for my grandchildren,
at that age.

Contents

Introduction

Some books are written because the author happens to be an expert in that field and wants to share his knowledge with the world at large; while some books are written because there is a commercial possibility; still others are written because the author feels a genuine need to express his ideas.

For me this book is important because I have gone through the problems that are associated with difficulties in remembering names and faces. For years, I struggled with the handicap, sometimes blaming the advancing age and at other times just making excuses. Then I realised that it was important to me, as a writer, to remember things. There were times when I wanted to quote a relevant quotation but couldn't recall the exact words. At other times, I struggled to remember a word, which I knew, was at the tip of my tongue but wouldn't surface when I wanted to use it. I couldn't remember faces and this caused me several embarrassing moments.

It hadn't always been this way. I was a fairly good student and could retain most of what I read. Somewhere along the line, I had stopped making an effort to remember what I read and this was causing the problems. There had been a time when I could solve pretty tough equations mentally. I had no problem converting the currency values when I went abroad. I did it without the use of pen and paper. I had an amazing memory for numbers. In fact, I rarely noted down phone numbers. You can well imagine how I must have felt when I realised that I could no longer recall important information. The current state of affairs was something akin to the rusting of equipment. For long, I had neglected the machinery and the results were very disturbing.

Then I told myself, "Enough is enough. It's time I do something about the problem and improve my memory." That was the turning point in my life. I ransacked the libraries for all books available on the subject; I attended several seminars on memory improvement; and I tried out various permutation and combinations of my own. I found that the techniques taught by the experts ran along familiar lines and were almost similar in nature. I also found that our ancient scriptures had a lot to offer on the subject, in an indirect manner. I discovered that Swami Vivekananda was an expert in memorising and speed-reading. I read several of his books and reached my own conclusions.

At the end of it all, I have realised that anyone can improve memory with a little effort and perseverance. Memory improvement techniques are pretty simple to learn but they require a lot of practice and constant use, otherwise there is hardly any benefit.

Whether one is a student or an executive, a homemaker or a businessman, a good memory is one thing that comes handy in everyone's life. Everyone wants to possess a good memory because it could make a tremendous difference to their lives. You, too, want to develop a fantastic memory.

This book is aimed at helping you hone up your recall system. If you feel that you could better your chances in life by acquiring a sharp memory, you must try to implement the ideas given in this book.

Some people like to say that they have a bad memory. They seem to be quite proud of the fact. While it may serve some absurd purpose to do so, I cannot but detect a sense of frustration in their mien. After all, no one is quite happy when one is unable to recall important information.

The good news is that anyone can have a good memory. It is not at all difficult to develop this particular faculty provided one makes a serious effort to achieve it.

I am writing this book to help those who are sailing in the same boat as me. Most of these techniques are tried and tested and are not difficult to follow, provided your intentions are serious. You could pass on these skills to your children and friends, for their benefit, once you have mastered them yourself.

But if you are one of those who buy a book on self-improvement and take it home with great enthusiasm, only to decorate the bookshelf, let me tell you something important –"the secret to any skill is the continuous use and practice". I suggest that you apply the techniques on a regular basis and you are sure to realise the difference within four to six months.

–Tanushree Podder

1. First the Fundamentals

The Brain and Memory Connection

No one is born with a poor memory. As human beings, we have been gifted with an amazingly powerful brain. And God has not been partial to anyone in making this extraordinary gift. We, however, often make fun of the forgetful people or people with poor memory and tease them by saying – "You must have been standing at the end of the queue when God was doling out the grey matter."

It is worthwhile to learn about the fantastic organ called brain, which governs most of our actions as well as thinking. It is like the master controller, rather like the remote control that you use to surf channels on the television. The brain is constantly bombarded with information, which is relayed through all our senses. Just imagine the enormous task it has in dealing with all this information, which is constantly being passed on to it.

How Does it Handle all the Traffic of Information?

The amount of information that floods in the brain is staggering. The brain has an unenviable job of sifting out the unimportant bits and selecting the important matters that need to be stored. Memory is just one of the facets of the multifarious functions of the brain. Since this book deals with memory, we will only discuss that facet of the brain function.

The human brain is a complex and highly developed organ. It consists of billions of cells that are constantly analysing, storing and retrieving information. No computer can match the efficient and organised functioning of a healthy brain. An interesting fact about the brain is that although it is just 2 percent of the total body weight, it uses up about 20 percent of the oxygen used by the entire body, when it is at rest. The brain cannot go without oxygen for more than 3-5 minutes without causing serious damage to it.

The most striking feature of the brain is the backup system. It stores each memory in a different slot. The memory system works in an amazing manner. Sometimes you will find that a certain odour brings back memories of your childhood or a visit to a hill station triggers a memory of a childhood vacation in another hill station. At other times, you may spend hours trying to recall someone's name without any success, only to remember the name suddenly when you are talking to someone or doing something else.

What is Memory?

Memory is the power of the brain to recall any information that has been stored in it. It is the power to remember something that has been learnt or experienced. Memory is important because if there was no memory, there would be no learning. We will forget things soon after learning them. We will not be able to recall any experience either.

The efficiency of the recall system is what makes your memory good or bad. As such, there is nothing like good memory and bad memory. It is just the matter of training your brain to recall efficiently.

Remembering is a process that must be learned, just like walking, talking, eating, differentiating colours, distinguishing sounds and telling time. You learned these things when you were a child and now you can perform them without effort, without even being conscious of the mental processes involved. You can learn the process of using your memory just as thoroughly, and when you do, you will have hundred times more power of knowledge and experience than what you have now.

Anyone can hone up the memory by training it. In order to make decisions and solve problems, one needs to refer to previous experiences. To refer to the previous experiences, we must remember them. No one really likes to waste time on re-learning. Therefore, it is imperative to improve our memory.

Ever since the time of Cicero, men have been developing techniques to improve memory. The fundamentals remain the same; only the modifications keep pace with the changing times.

How does Memory Work?

Psychologists have classified the stages of memory process into three main categories. They call them – sensory memory, short-term memory, and long-term memory.

Sensory memory is a very fleeting type of memory, which works only as long as the experience is present. For instance, if you were looking at a bird, you would remember it only as long as it is in front of you. The moment it flies away, you would not be able to remember what it looked like unless you have filed the information away into your short-term memory. In effect, sensory memory holds as long as your senses are experiencing a thing. Whether it is the feel of an object, smell or the sensation of anything, it is all there in the sensory memory for a very brief period while your sense is active.

Short-term memory, on the other hand, can help you recall for a little longer; in fact, as long as you keep thinking about it. Whether it is the telephone number that you have been repeating constantly till you write it down, or the image of the bird, it will remain available as long as you actively think about it. Otherwise, it will be erased within a span of about 20 seconds. To remember, the brain has to transfer it into the long-term memory bracket.

How does the long-term memory work? It is the mainstay of the memory system and can hold unlimited amount of information, which can range from a few minutes old to life-time period. Long-term memory is like a huge hard disk of a giant computer where unlimited information can be stored for a lifetime. It is this memory that we have to hone, polish and activate.

All this sounds pretty technical and complicated but just think of it in terms of storage tricks. Take the example of an ice-cream. You can't keep the ice-cream from melting beyond a few minutes, if you do not keep it in the fridge. Sensory memory is like the ice-cream kept outside. If you keep the ice-cream in the fridge, it will remain in the semi-formed state and that is the short-term memory. Now, put the ice-cream in the freezer and it will harden to a large extent. Even if you take it out and keep it outside, it will take some time to melt. This is the long-term memory. Quite simple, isn't it?

In this book we will try to learn the process by which we can make efforts towards transferring information into the long-term memory shelf of our brain, so that the information remains embedded in our brain and our memory improves.

Just getting information is not enough; it has to be retrieved on demand. Whether it is a student, homemaker, businessman or an executive, everyone needs to recall some kind of information.

If you are a student, think how fantastic it would be if you could remember everything that is taught in the class and recall it all efficiently during the examination.

If you are a homemaker, imagine the euphoria of remembering all details of household expenses, bills, the amount paid, shopping list etc.

If you are a businessman, just think of the benefits of knowing all the facts about your business on your fingertips.

And if you are a marketing executive, can you imagine the impression you can make on your boss if you were to reel out all the sales figures at a moment's notice?

Why just the student, businessman, and the homemaker, memory is a very important aspect of life which affects every human being.

Back in 1885, the German scientist Herman Ebbinghaus made the first experimental studies in the field of memory. What he discovered then holds true even today. He found that by using the common method of memorising, we forget 40 percent within twenty minutes and 75 percent by the end of the week. Doesn't it stand to reason, then, that if you are going to bother to learn things once, you might as well go to a little extra trouble and memorise it forever? You can do this easily by repeating briefly what you have learned once a day for a week, and then once a week for a month.

There have been men with a genius for memory, but their feats lie entirely outside the experience of us, ordinary mortals. Lord Macaulay could memorise entire books at a single reading. Mozart as a boy wrote down the score of an oratorio after hearing it once. Closer home, we had Swami Vivekananda who could duplicate the feats of Lord Macaulay.

Story goes that, one day, Swami Vivekananda was waiting for a friend in a room. During the period of waiting, he picked up a book that was lying there and began reading it. Ten minutes later, when the friend appeared, he suggested that Vivekananda read the book because it was a very good one. Vivekananda told him that he had already finished reading it and could quote facts from the book verbatim. The friend was amazed at Vivekananda's prowess but it was quite a simple feat for Vivekananda who possessed a photographic memory.

TIP – The mind has an endless capacity.

Selective Memory

Have you noticed how you can recall certain events and things in lucid details, while some of the more important happenings may simply escape your memory? For instance, you may be able to remember the face and name of your kindergarten friend but the name and face of a business client, introduced just a couple of days back, eludes you. You need to check the visiting card to remember his name. You may distinctly recall one particular holiday of your childhood, while a more recent one doesn't pop up so easily in your mind.

Another example is the fact that most of us can remember even the words used by a person during a quarrel, years after the incident. We can remember specific instances when someone rebuked us, insulted us or hurt us. We can usually remember these incidents because we want to remember them. We feel emotionally connected to those incidents. We love remembering the tragic times because we want to wallow in self-pity. We love recalling each and every moment of the special incident when we were given a special honour. These are just some of the examples of super memory and super recall.

Now the question remains that if we can do it for some incidents and events, why can't we do it for all events and incidents.

What is the reason for such lapses? Why do we recall selectively? The reason is quite simple really. We tend to forget a person or an event just because we don't make enough effort to remember them. This should convince you that if you can recall one incident, you could recall many others. This should also make you realise that we are all capable of remembering things if we make adequate efforts to remember them.

TIP – Anyone can have a powerful memory.

The Theory of Use and Disuse

An average human being loses up to 1,00,000 brain cells every day due to disuse. Unlike the other cells of our body, the brain cells do not multiply. Any cells that are damaged or not used, simply degenerate. By the age of 35 a human being loses over 1,000 nerve cells a day.

The lesser a person uses his brain, the worse his memory becomes. People get mentally out of shape when they stop challenging their minds; this happens when they opt for habitual solutions rather than purposeful thought, or if they confine their thinking to a small range of interests. Remember that mental fitness - your ability to concentrate, to reason, to visualise, to imagine, to make decisions, to solve problems and to think creatively - depends greatly on how well and how often you exercise your mind. You need to exercise all of your mental muscles in order to keep yourself mentally fit. Just like several body muscles work together to create physical movement, several mental muscles work together to create clear, purposeful thinking.

TIP – Fitness of mind is as important as that of the body.

Remember the Positive and Forget the Negative

The mind has an amazing capacity. In fact, there are no limits to its power. The power of mind can be extended to a limitless extent. It is said that Lucius Scipio could remember the names of all the people who lived in Rome during his time. There are teachers who know the names of all the children in the class and even those not in their class. Imagine remembering the names of a few hundred children studying in various classes. If a teacher can remember hundreds of names, can't you remember an equivalent number?

Remembering the relevant bits of information is necessary but it is neither advisable nor possible to retain each and every piece of information that our brain receives during our lifetime.

So What does One Do?

We simply remove the ones that are not relevant and retain the ones that are useful.

We know that we cannot possibly remember nor want to remember everything. To make our memories serve us intelligently, we have to be able to choose the things we want to remember and concentrate on developing selective type of memory. It is worth remembering two fundamental rules –

- Everyone has greater power of memory than he imagines.
- Although intensive training produces great improvement in memory, training does not develop the general faculty of memory but simply increases the particular kind of memory job that is practised.

So, to develop your memory in order to increase your personal efficiency you must first choose the kind of remembering on which you want to concentrate. If you learn to memorise poetry effectively, your friends may consider you more cultured and you may get extra enjoyment out of life, but it will not help you remember the grocery list.

To help you decide what kind of memory you want to cultivate, you must decide the kind of things that you need to remember and concentrate on them.

Why should we try to recall unpleasant little episodes, which •prey on our minds? Why should we torture ourselves with the tragic incidents that happened in our lives? Why not clear the junk to accommodate more useful information?

The mind is like an endless shelf. We are constantly heaping information on it, just like we stack clothes in the cupboard. What happens when we need a specific dress that we want to wear for the special party in the evening? We spend a whole lot of time, searching for the specific dress amidst the chaotic clutter. Similarly, the mind, which is heaped with a whole lot of irrelevant and useless information, takes time to dredge up the necessary information. Sometimes it even fails to retrieve the useful stuff.

TIP – **Unclutter your mind. Keep the positive information and junk the negative ones.**

Why do We Forget?

Can you Recall your Passport Number?

I bet you can't. Simply, because it is not used everyday. You will have to make a big effort to seek it out from the bottom of the stack of information that is stored in your brain. To be remembered easily, information needs to be organized and meaningful, and needs to come to us at a slow pace so as to process it.

The reason for most of the annoying instances of forgetting is that you do not take the trouble to connect new information with some fact you already know. Isolated facts drop out of the mind quickly, but if you file new knowledge in relation to something already established in your mind, you will retain it and be able to refer to it whenever you need it. It is simply a matter of making special use of your power of association, which is the beginning of all learning processes.

In mental terms, the more you associate a fact with other stored information in your mind, the better your memory can retain it. Each of its associates becomes a hook on which the new information hangs. Association is making mental hook from which you may fish facts out of your mind, as you require them. The mental filing system will provide the mental hooks upon which to hang, or file, anything you want to remember. Certain selected words, called Key Words, are the mental hooks in your filing system. Each one of these represents a vivid image.

Let us see what reasons the scientists have attributed to the habit of forgetting. The scientific theory is that people forget more as time passes. This makes sense. I can recall the dress I wore in the morning quite easily, but I take time in remembering the dress I wore yesterday morning. And if you ask me what I was wearing last Sunday morning, I will have a little problem recalling the dress.

According to the scientists, we forget things because of certain processes. These processes are:

- Interference
- Retrieval failure
- Motivated forgetting
- Constructive process

I think we should understand what these terms are all about so that we don't get confused about them when someone tries to use them to impress. Since we will be spending quite some time and energy wanting and trying to improve memory, we might as well do a thorough job.

What is Interference?

Simply speaking, when there is problem with the recall of an event because there is some other event that interferes, it is called **interference**. The learning of a new fact may sometimes interfere with the memory of a similar fact learned earlier. Let us make it easier. If you bought a new vehicle and tried to remember the registration number of this vehicle, you are likely to find that the registration number of your old vehicle keeps popping up in your mind. This is interference. But after a few months when you have learnt the new registration number, you may find it difficult to remember the old one. This is also interference.

What is Retrieval Failure?

It happens to all of us at some point of time or the other. We are in the midst of a conversation and the talk hovers around the works of a famous author, e.g. Eric Berne. You may have read the books written by him and want to tell your friends about it. You have the name of the book on the tip of our tongue but it wouldn't surface. Hours later, it suddenly pops up in your memory system. This temporary loss of memory is known as retrieval failure. It is like trying to find a specific dress in a pile of other clothes. You just can't find it immediately, but will locate it eventually.

What is Motivated Forgetting?

Motivated forgetting is about the things we want to block out from memory. If we don't want to recall a particular unpleasant episode of our life, we simply block it and won't remember it. This is also known as repression.

Constructive Process

There is another word that is generally bandied about by the experts. It is refabrication or confabulation. When you have a hazy memory of an event, you try to fill in the missing information with probable details in order to complete the picture. It is like the jigsaw puzzle where a minor piece is missing so you fit in something similar to complete the puzzle. This is called confabulation. You actually recreate the event by fitting in the missing link while retaining most of the facts.

TIP – **Associate and organise.**   OO

2. The Process of Remembering

At this stage, you may well ask – "Alright, I have realised the importance of remembering, I have also learnt the need to unclutter the mind. But how can I remember things?"

The first step towards improving your recall system is to observe. The stronger the observation the better is the memory. Most of us do not attach enough importance to the power of observation. As a result we often overlook details while observing. A simple test of your observation would be to try and recall specifics after you have watched a movie. For instance, try to remember the dress worn by the heroine while singing a specific song or the locale that went in the background.

You will find that you will not be able to recall these details initially, but as you hone up your power of observation, you will be able to remember the minutest of the details. The reason for this change is very simple. You have been able to improve your power of remembering because you have made your observation keener.

Our forefathers had a much better memory than we do. Since there were no written scriptures, much of the text was passed from generation to generation through oral communication. For this, the learned few had to memorise the entire lot of scriptures through the rote method. It was much later that writing methods were discovered and the ancient wisdom and scriptures were put in writing.

No doubt that the observation power of the people in the ancient times was also keen since they had to remember everything without being able to put it in writing.

Why is it Important to Observe?

Have you ever wondered why the people, who possess good memories, have a very good power of observation, too? The reason

18

is quite simple. It is the observation power, which makes their memory good.

How can One Increase the Observation Power?

To be able to observe better, you need to be attentive and focussed. If you are not attentive, you can't be observant and if you are not observant you can't have a good memory. There are various ways to strengthen the observation. You can begin playing the memory games that are flooding the markets these days. The games like 'jigsaw puzzles' and 'spot the differences' are also very effective in increasing the power of observation.

Give yourself some simple observation tasks every day. For instance, if you are going for a party, observe the dresses worn by five people. When you return home, try to recapitulate the details. Increase the number to ten, after a few days. Similarly, while driving, when you halt at the traffic light you can try to observe the vehicles around you. Note the kind of vehicle, the colour and the make of the vehicle, the driver and the passengers. Try and recall these when you reach your office. While shopping for detergents try and observe how many brands of detergents are available at the supermarket, what is the difference in the packing, the prices, etc. etc. These exercises will hone up your observation within a few weeks.

TIP – Focused Attention = Powerful Observation = Effective Recall

The Memory Process

What constitutes the memory process? Just like every other function, memory is a series of things happening one after the other.

There are three fundamental questions related to the memory process.

How are Memories Formed?

Through the process of 'Encoding'.

How are Memories Retained?

Through the process of 'Storage'.

How are Memories Recalled?

Through the process of 'Retrieval'.

The process of remembering can actually be divided into four easy steps:

- Attention and Selection
- Encoding
- Storage
- Retrieval

Attention and Selection

It has already been established that attention plays a very important role in memory. In fact, the first process of memory is attention. There is much more information in your environment than you can process at any one time. All our senses are absorbing a multitude of information from various sources and all this needs to be processed. At any given time, our brain is exposed to hundreds of messages that need its attention. But it can't process all these messages at the same time.

Thus, you must make choices regarding the stimuli to which you will attend. The choices can be conscious and unconscious. Imagine two friends who are driving to Goa for holiday. Both have different plans for how they want to spend their vacation: one listening to local bands, the other surfing and swimming.

They stop to eat at a roadside café. During the halt they are approached by a stranger who asks if they know of a shop selling surfing gear, located close-by. Assuming they passed one on the way to the cafe, the chances are that the surfer, but not his friend, would have remembered seeing it. Had the stranger asked about music clubs, you might find the opposite scenario.

The conclusion is that each of them attended to what was of individual interest. The idea here is to emphasize the roles attention and selection play in our memory.

Encoding

Once something is attended to, it must be encoded to be remembered. Basically, encoding refers to translating incoming information into a mental representation that can be stored in memory.

You can encode the same information in a number of different ways. For example, you can encode information according to its sound (acoustic code), what it looks like (visual code), or what it means (semantic code).

Suppose, for example, that you are trying to remember these three types of encoding from your notes. You might say each of the terms aloud and encode the sounds of the words (acoustic), you might see the three types of encoding on your page and visualize the way the words look (visual), or you might think about the meanings of each of the terms (semantic).

How does encoding apply to memory? Well, the way you encode information may affect what you remember and how you recall it later. If you encode the three things visually or acoustically, but not semantically, you may be able to list them during a test, but you may have difficulty in recalling what each term means. If you encode them only semantically, you might be able to explain what they mean but have difficulty remembering the order in which they were listed on the page.

You may be able to remember information best if you use techniques (while retrieving the information) that are related to the way you have encoded it. For example, if you encode something visually, you will be able to recall it most easily by drawing on visual cues. You will find that many of the memory techniques discussed in this book are designed to help you encode the information in different ways.

Storage

Storage is the process of holding information in your memory. A distinction is often made between short-term and long-term memory. Short-term memory is just that, brief and transient. Think about looking up a new phone number in the phone book and making a call. You may remember it long enough to make the call, but do not recall it later. This is your short-term memory, which can hold a small amount of information for a short period of time. Once you stop attending to the number, perhaps after you make the call and move on to another task, you are likely to forget it. In order to remember the number for a longer period of time (and after attending to other things), you would need to store it in your long-term memory.

The transfer of information from short- to long-term memory can be achieved in many ways. Simply repeating the information can help if it is repeated enough times. For example, frequently called phone numbers are remembered because you have used (repeated) the number many times.

Although simply repeating, or practising something can help move it into long-term memory, another strategy for transferring information is to think about it deeply. That is, elaborate on the information, drawing connections between what you are trying to remember and the other things with which you are already familiar. You might learn that telephone number quicker, for example, if you notice that it includes the dates of your friend's birthday, the numbers on your license plate, or some other familiar number pattern.

For instance, if the phone number that you want to remember happens to be 224 7450, break it up into three or four parts e.g. 2 24 74 50. Now, if your date of birth is 24th February, it connects with the first three digits. The last two can be associated as half a century and if you add 24 and 50, you get the number 74. There are many ways to work this out and you must select the one that works best for you.

Retrieval

In terms of memory improvement, it can help to understand how the retrieval process relates to encoding and storage. Consider the relationship between retrieval and encoding. If you have encoded something visually, but are trying to retrieve it acoustically, you will have difficulty remembering it. Like encoding, information can be retrieved through visualizing it, thinking about the meaning, or imagining the sound, etc.

The more ways information has been encoded, the more ways there are for retrieving it. Imagine that you are taking a test in which you are given a definition and asked to recall the word it describes. You may recall the page of your notes that the word was on and visualize the word, or you might say the definition to yourself and remember yourself repeating the word. This shows that memory is aided by encoding and retrieving information in multiple ways. The more methods of encoding you use, the better will be the retrieval.

Retrieval relates to storage as well. Obviously the memory has to be stored in order for you to retrieve it, but knowing how it was stored can help. This is where elaboration and processing come in. When attempting to retrieve information, it helps to think about related ideas.

For example, you are trying to remember the details of an important meeting you attended on a specific date. Although you are able to visualize the setting of the meeting, you cannot recall the people who attended it. You do remember, however, that the same people attended a lunch together, after the meeting. As you think about the lunch, you visualise the seating arrangement and are able to recall the faces. This is one reason why intentionally organizing information in your memory when you are learning it helps you recall it later.

TIP – Attention ——> Encoding ——> Storage ——> Retrieval

These are the steps of memory discussed thus far. First, you select the information to which you will attend. You then encode the information for storage (where it can be practised and processed more deeply). Later, when needed, information is retrieved by using a search strategy that parallels how the information was encoded and stored.

Why do We Forget Despite Attempts at Remembering?

Although information can be stored in long-term memory for extended periods of time, "memory decay" does take place. In other words, we can forget what we learn. In fact, we forget things shortly after we learn them. This has two implications in terms of improving our memory. First, as disheartening as it is, you often learn a great deal more than you can retain in the long run.

But, before you lose heart entirely, keep in mind that the memories can be retained with a little effort. So, the second implication for improving memory involves maintaining memories with the least amount of effort. In order to retain information in memory, you must practise, think about, and sometimes relearn things. Every time you practise and relearn the information, you are reinforcing it in your memory.

Taking a few moments to do frequent, but brief, reviews will save your time by helping you retain what you have learned. For example, if you are reading an important document, it's a good idea to make rehearsal part of your reading and note-taking regimen. When you complete one page, take a few minutes to rehearse the material as a way of moving the information from short-term to long-term memory. Not that this practice alone is sufficient to recall all the details, but it will enhance your understanding and recall of the document.

TIP – Memory *'Mantras'* : Observe, Associate, File away.

○ ○

3. How to Improve Memory

Attempts to improve memory are not new. For centuries, man has been trying out ways and means to improve his memory because he has realised the importance of having a good memory. Mnemonics, a method still used for efficient memory, was devised by the Greeks a long long time ago.

While there are many methods that keep appearing from time to time; there are some, which have proved their efficacy. They remain popular because of the ease and practicality of implementing them. Of these, mnemonic, link system and pegging are the most popular.

One thing that needs to be mentioned here is that there are no quick fix methods available for improving memory. These methods have to be practised with sincerity and regularity in order to apply them effectively. Just as with any self-improvement process, memory improvement needs consistent efforts and takes a little time to make an impact. So, don't expect overnight results or you will be disappointed!

Memory Improvement Techniques

Mnemonics

The Ancient Greeks developed basic memory systems called Mnemonics, a name derived from their Goddess of Memory, Mnemosene. In the ancient world, a trained memory was an immense asset, particularly in public life. There were no convenient devices for taking notes, and early Greek orators delivered long speeches with great accuracy because they learned the speeches using Mnemonic systems.

The Greeks discovered that human memory is largely an Associative process - which works by linking things together. For example, think of a pineapple. The moment your brain registers the word 'pineapple'; it recalls the shape, colour, taste, texture and smell of that fruit. All these things are associated in your memory with the word 'pineapple'. Any thought, action, word, statement, or whatever, can trigger another, associated memory. When you recall what you had for lunch yesterday, that may remind you of something someone said during lunch, which may recall the memory of some background music which was playing, which may evoke something which occurred ten years ago, and this can go on and on. These associations do not have to be logical - they can be completely random or absurd. In fact, the more absurd the association, the better the recall.

Association, Imagination and Location

The three fundamental principles underlying the use of mnemonics are:

- Association
- Imagination
- Location

Working together, these principles can be used to generate powerful mnemonic systems. Once you have absorbed and applied these techniques you will understand how to design and apply these principles to your field and to devise your own powerful, sophisticated recall systems.

Association

Association is the method by which you link a thing to be remembered with something personal. Although I am outlining some associations to you, it is much better to formulate your own associations as they reflect the way in which your mind works.

What you need to remember is that things can be associated by:

- Being placed on top of the associated object
- Crashing or penetrating into each other
- Merging together

- Wrapping around each other
- Rotating around each other or dancing together
- Having the same colour, smell, shape, or feeling

An associated image is the image that you visualise and connect with the item you are trying to remember.

For example: if the number 1 item on your shopping list was goldfish, visualising a 1-shaped spear being used to spear a goldfish to feed a starving family will link the number 1 with a goldfish.

The Principle of Association forms the basis of all the memory systems. The principle is: **"You can remember any new information if you associate it to something you already know or remember."**

Most of us have actually used this principle of association all our lives, even though we might have done so subconsciously. Do you remember the shape of Austria, Canada, Belgium, or Germany? Probably not.

What about Italy? If you remember the shape of Italy, it is because you've been told at some time that Italy is shaped like a boot. You made an association with something already known - the shape of a boot, and Italy's shape couldn't be forgotten once you had made this association. Biology students have used the slipper shape to remember the shape of a Paramecium.

There are many other common uses of the Principle of Association. Students are told to think of VIBGYOR (Violet, Indigo, Blue, Green, Yellow, Orange and Red), in order to help remember the colours of the rainbow. Most of us have used BODMAS (Bracket, Off, Divide, Multiply, Add, Subtract), to remember the sequence of solving maths equations.

All these examples of association are limited to the extent that they work only for one specific thing. When you have learnt how to associate consciously anything you want to remember to something you already know, then you will have a trained memory. It is really as simple as that.

An Exercise

For your first exercise in Association, let's assume you want to memorise these 10 unrelated items in sequence: banana, car, newspaper, sausage, pen, tree, watch, tie, television, and football. In order to do this, you are going to consciously apply the basic memory rule defined earlier, but with an important addition - **You can remember any new information if you associate it to something you already know in some ludicrous way.**

First, picture a banana in your mind. You can't apply the rule yet. Now we come to the next item - car. If we assume that you already know banana, you can now apply the memory rule. You simply need to create a ridiculous picture, or image, in your mind's eye - an association between banana and car.

In order to do this you need a ridiculous, far-fetched, crazy, illogical and absurd picture or image to associate the two items. What you don't want is a logical or sensible picture. For example, a sensible picture might be someone sitting in a car eating a banana. Although this would not be something you would expect to see every day, it is in not in any way bizarre or impossible.

An impossible, crazy, picture might be - a gigantic banana is driving a car along the motorway, or you open a car door and billions of bananas tumble out and knock you over. These are ludicrous, illogical pictures. What you need to do is select one of these pictures, or a crazy image you thought of yourself, and see it in your mind for just a fraction of a second. Be careful not to picture the words 'banana' and 'car'. You need to see the action you've selected - the huge banana driving the car, or the mountain of bananas tumbling out of a car, or whichever image you've decided on. See that picture in your mind's eye for just an instant, right now.

The next item on your list is newspaper. Assuming that you already remember car, you now need to form a ridiculous association in your mind between car and newspaper. For example, you open a newspaper and a car leaps out of the pages and knocks you over. Or you are driving a huge rolled up newspaper instead of a car. Or you are driving a car when a massive sheet of newspaper appears in front of you, which the car rips as you drive through it. Choose one of these images, or one you conjured up yourself, and picture it clearly for a split second.

Sausage is the next item to remember, so you now need to form a ludicrous association between newspaper and sausage. You could picture yourself eating rolled up newspapers and eggs for breakfast instead of sausages and eggs, or you are reading a gigantic sausage which has lots of news printed on it, or a paperboy is walking along a street pushing very long sausages through letterboxes instead of newspapers. See one of those crazy images. Next on the list is pen. Associate it to sausage. See yourself trying to write with a sausage instead of a pen, or you cut into a sausage with a knife and fork and gallons of ink shoot out of the sausage into your face. Picture one of these scenarios clearly in your mind.

The next item is tree. Picture millions of pens growing on a tree instead of leaves, or a colossal fountain pen is growing in your garden instead of a tree. Be sure to see the image clearly. Watch is the next item on the list. Picture a tree with lots of branches which are wearing giant wristwatches, or you look at your watch and see that there is a tree growing out of it, with roots curling up your arm. Select one of these images, or one of your own, and see it for an instant in your mind's eye.

Tie comes next. See yourself wearing an elongated wristwatch instead of a tie, or an enormously long tie is tied around your wrist instead of a watch, so long that it drags along the floor. The next item to be remembered is television. You might picture yourself with a television hanging around your neck instead of a tie, or you switch on the television and a vast, horribly spotted tie bursts out of the screen, unrolling itself for yards and yards. Select a crazy association between tie and television, and see the picture in your mind. The final item on the list is football. See a football match where the players are kicking around a television instead of a football. Or you are watching a football game on television when millions of footballs suddenly burst through the screen and hit you in the face. Picture one of those images.

If you have really tried to see all those pictures, you will now remember the list of ten items in sequence, both forwards and backwards. Try it now. If you miss one or two, simply go back over the list and strengthen your associations.

Imagination

Imagination is used to create the links and associations needed to create effective memory techniques. Confusing? Well, let me try and put it in a simple manner. Imagination is the way in which you use your mind to create the links that have the most meaning for you. Images that I create will have less power and impact for you, because they reflect the way in which I think. To have a stronger impact, you have to visualise and imagine your own images.

The more strongly you imagine and visualise a situation, the more effectively it will stick in your mind for later recall. Mnemonic imagination can be as violent, vivid, or sensual as you like, as long as it helps you remember what needs to be remembered. You have already seen in the example given earlier as to how it works, and you must have already tried it out, too.

Location

Location provides you with two things: a coherent context into which information can be placed so that it hangs together, and a way of separating one mnemonic from another: e.g. by setting one mnemonic in one place, I can separate it from a similar mnemonic located in another place.

Location provides context and texture to your mnemonics, and prevents them from being confused with similar mnemonics. For example, by setting one mnemonic with visualisations in the city of Uttar Pradesh in India and another similar mnemonic with images of New York or Tokyo allows us to separate them with no danger of confusion.

So using the three fundamentals of Association, Imagination and Location you can design images that strongly link things between themselves and with other things, so that it allows you to recall those images in a way that does not conflict with other images and associations.

Using Mnemonics More Effectively

When you are creating a mnemonic, e.g. an image or story to remember a telephone number, the following things can be used to make the mnemonic more memorable:

- Use positive, pleasant images. The brain often blocks out unpleasant ones.
- Exaggerate the size of important parts of the image.
- Use humour! Funny or peculiar things are easier to remember than normal ones.

- Similarly rude or sexual rhymes are very difficult to forget!
- Symbols (e.g. red traffic lights, pointing fingers, etc.) can be used in mnemonics.
- Vivid, colourful images are easier to remember than drab ones.
- Use all the senses to code information or dress up an image. Remember that your mnemonic can contain sounds, smells, tastes, touch, movements and feelings as well as pictures.
- Bringing three dimensions and movement to an image makes it more vivid. Movement can be used either to maintain the flow of association, or can help to remember actions.
- Locate similar mnemonics in different places with backgrounds of those places. This will help in maintaining similar images distinct and unconfused.

The important thing is that the mnemonic should clearly relate to the thing being remembered, and that it should be vivid enough to be clearly recalled whenever you think about it.

TIP – Association, Imagination and Location are the keys to successful Mnemonics.

The Link System

The Link Method is one of the easiest mnemonic techniques available, but is very powerful as well. However, it is not quite as reliable as a peg technique, because images are not tied to specific, inviolable sequences. The Linking method is a permanent memory method and is a very easy method to master. It functions quite simply by making associations between things in a list, often as a story. The flow of the story and the strength of the visualisations of the images provide the cues for retrieval.

The Link System can be used to memorise any information, which has to be learned in sequence. Speeches, presentations, stories, jokes, recipes, and formulas are all examples of things, which must be learned in sequence. The most common problem experienced by people trying to learn the Link System is to make their mental pictures sufficiently ridiculous to make strong and memorable associations. It does take a certain amount of imagination to form ridiculous pictures in your mind. Children have no trouble in forming silly or absurd pictures - they do it naturally.

Unfortunately, as we grow up, most of us tend to use our imagination lesser and lesser, and so it becomes a little rusty.

However, that capacity for imagination we had when we were children is still there - it just needs a little bit of greasing and oiling. Applying the systems given in this book will automatically provide the exercise that your imagination needs. So don't worry if at first you have to apply some effort to create those ludicrous mental pictures. After a little practice, you'll find that you can do it quickly and easily!

Five Principles to Help You

There are five basic principles you can apply in forming your mental pictures, which will help you make your associations strong and long lasting. These are quite similar to the ones suggested in the mnemonic system.

1. **Out of Proportion** – In all your images, try to distort size and shape. In the first exercise, you were told to picture a 'Huge' sausage or a 'Gigantic' tie. Conversely, you can make things microscopically small.

2. **Substitution** – In the first exercise, we suggested that you visualise footballers kicking a television around a football pitch instead of a football, or pens growing on a tree instead of leaves. Substituting an out of place item in an image increases the probability of recall.

3. **Exaggeration** – Try to picture vast quantities in your images. For example, we used the word 'billions' (of bananas).

4. **Movement** – Any movement or action is always easy to remember. For example, we suggested that you saw yourself cutting a sausage and gallons of ink squirting out and hitting you in the face.

5. **Humour** – The funnier, more absurd and zany you can make your images, the more memorable they will be.

Applying any combination of these five principles when forming your images will help make your mental associations truly outstanding and memorable. At first you may find that you need to consciously apply one or more of the five principles in order to make your pictures sufficiently ludicrous. After a little practice however, you should find that applying the principles becomes an automatic and natural process.

An Exercise

Your second memory training exercise again involves memorising a list of items in sequence, but this time we'll make the list more practical.

Assume you wish to memorise the following shopping list of fifteen items:

Chicken, Pumpkin, Detergent Powder, Cornflakes, Milk, Tomato Sauce, Shampoo, Green Peas, Pastry, Car Polish, Newspaper, Bread Loaf, Tea Bags, Soap, and Eggs.

Of course, it's just as easy to jot down your shopping lists on a piece of paper, as it is to try and memorise it. But how many times have you reached the supermarket or shops only to realise that you've left your list on the kitchen table, or in the pocket of a dress, which you decided not to wear after all?

Any way, let's assume for the moment that you wish to memorise the above list of items. You are going to memorise the list of items in sequence, using the Link System. Of course, it is not important to know a shopping list in sequence - you simply want to remember all the items. But, if you don't memorise the list in sequence, and particularly if it's a long list, how else will you be sure you've remembered all the items? (Actually, there is another method of memorising all the items, using the Peg System, but we'll come to that later!)

O.K., let's begin with the exercise of memorising the above-mentioned shopping list. The first item is Chicken. Before moving on to item two, consider for a moment how you can be sure that you will remember the first item in any Link. After all, there is nothing to associate it to. The answer is to associate it to the subject of your Link - in this case the supermarket. For example, picture yourself opening the supermarket door and millions of chickens flying out, knocking you over. If you can picture that ridiculous image, or a similar ludicrous picture clearly in your mind for just an instant, then you will remember that first item on your shopping list.

An alternative method of remembering the first item of any Link is to think of any item in the middle of the Link, and work backwards through your associations. This must eventually lead you to your first item. For the moment, let's assume that you know the first item, chicken. The second item is pumpkin. Now, form a

33

ridiculous association between chicken and pumpkin. You might picture a chicken trying to lay a huge pumpkin instead of an egg, with a contorted expression on its face. This is rather a crude picture, but one that is likely to stay in your mind. See that image, or a similar zany association between chicken and pumpkin in your mind's eye, right now. Remember that the ludicrous associations suggested here are only suggestions. If you come up with your own images then so much the better - you are increasing your Initial Awareness.

Now, continue with your Link. The next item is detergent powder, so you might picture yourself trying to wash some clothes in the washing machine and instead of the detergent powder you have put a gigantic pumpkin in the washing machine. As you start the washing machine, the pumpkin breaks into a million pieces and the seeds scatter all over the clothes.

Next comes the packet of cornflakes. To associate that item to the previous one, you could picture yourself adding detergent in milk, instead of water and you can also see the white frothy bubbles floating all around the house, in your mind.

The fifth item is milk. You might picture yourself pouring from a milk bottle, but instead of milk out come hundreds of cornflakes. See each one of those cornflakes squeezing itself painfully out of the bottle, so that it bursts into a thousand pieces when it finally squeezes through the neck of the bottle.

Next comes the tomato sauce. Imagine yourself piercing the cap of the tomato sauce bottle, when gallons of milk squirt out, soaking you from head to toe.

The seventh item is shampoo. Picture yourself pouring some shampoo over your head, but instead of shampoo, a whole lot of tomato sauce comes squirting out of the bottle, until you are knee deep in the red mess. The next item is green peas; so associate that item to shampoo. You could see yourself lathering your hair with shampoo, when dozens of green peas suddenly start sprouting out of your hair. See that association, or one you thought of yourself, for just a split second. Remember, you don't have to see the picture for a long period of time - you just need to see it clearly for a fraction of a second.

You are now just over half way through forming your Link of fifteen items. Before continuing, just pause and review the associations you have made so far. Look back over the associations suggested up to this point, and consider how the five principles of Out of Proportion, Substitution, Exaggeration, Movement, and Humour have been used in the suggested images.

O.K., let's continue with the ninth item in the Link, pastry. To form a ludicrous association with green peas, you might see yourself cutting into a pastry with a knife and fork. Suddenly a huge green peas plant sprouts out of the middle of the pastry, so tall that it shoots right through the ceiling.

Next comes car polish. See yourself trying to clean a car with a pastry, instead of a tin of car polish. Picture yourself dipping a cloth into that pastry, and covering the car with the icing. See that image clearly.

The eleventh item is the newspaper. A zany association here might be - you open the newspaper to the middle pages, and an arm holding a duster covered in car polish zooms out of the newspaper and polishes your face, causing you to splutter and cough. Next, associate the newspaper to bread loaf. For example, imagine yourself trying to make sandwiches out of the newspaper, instead of the bread loaf.

Then come tea bags. A ridiculous picture here could be - you are trying to push a gigantic bread loaf into a teapot. The fourteenth item on your shopping list is soap. See yourself perhaps washing your face with tea bags, and getting into an awful mess. To complete your Link, associate soap to eggs. You could picture yourself eating a bar of soap out of an eggcup for breakfast, instead of a boiled egg. As you eat the soap out of the eggcup, your mouth fills up with soapsuds!

If you have really seen all those crazy pictures in your mind's eye, you will now know the shopping list in sequence, both forwards and backwards. As stated earlier, there's no reason why you would want to know the list in sequence, but it's an extremely useful exercise in practising the techniques of Association and Linking.

Now test yourself by writing down the fifteen items on a sheet of paper, both forwards and backwards.

In Association of ideas you were forming Links of items, which had no logical connection. The system works even better when you apply it to lists of items for a practical reason. If you really want to remember a particular list of items, then you will concentrate on it harder - your Initial Awareness will be increased. Make an effort to try some Links over the next few days. If you find linking fifteen items fairly easy, then try Linking thirty, or more. Once you have mastered the basic technique, there is no limit to the number of items you can Link in this way.

The Two Approaches to Link Method

In Link Method, you can use two approaches – the pure linking or the story method. The above example was just pure linking but you can weave a story around the items to make the learning more interesting and permanent.

Although it is possible to remember lists of words where each word is just associated with the next, it is often best to fit the associations into a story: otherwise by forgetting just one association, the entire list goes out of mind.

The Story Method

Given the fluid structure of this mnemonic, it is important that the images stored in your mind are as vivid as possible. Significantly, coding images are much stronger than those which merely support the flow of the story. Adding images to the story expands this technique. However, this system has its own limitation; after a certain number of images, the system may start to break down.

Purpose

The main purpose of the story method is to remember a list of objects, however long, in a certain order, and to be able to recall them in the same order, or even reverse order.

How it Works

It is done by inventing a **story** to link each item in the list to the next in the form of a chain.

Method

The best way to illustrate how incredibly simple but efficient this method is, I am going to provide a list of seemingly unrelated objects, and show you how to invent a silly story to connect them all together. When I thought of this list, I did not even think about how to link them together but it wasn't difficult, at all, to weave a story around the list. Here it is:

- Book, scissors, cat, butterfly, cheque, horse, sausage, mirror, videotape, flowerpot, microwave, tree, garden hose, joystick.
- I think you would agree that to remember this list in the correct order requires a definite plan of action.

Here is the story I made up to link them together:

I was reading a very interesting **book** in bed last night. It was a magic-trick book, because the pages had been hollowed out to contain a pair of **scissors**.

The pair of scissors had a mind of its own, because it was chasing a longhaired **cat** to give it a trim. The cat was pawing at a **butterfly**, which had peculiar wings made out of a large **cheque**. As I watched, the cheque floated down and rested across a **horse**.

The horse was particularly enjoying eating a large shiny **sausage**. The sausage was shining like a mirror.

The mirror was in the shape of those copyright protection holograms you get on **videotapes**. It was very large videotape, because one of the spools supported a **flowerpot**, and it was spinning wildly.

The pot was rather cold, so I put it in the **microwave** to heat it up. As I opened the door to the microwave, it became a door in the bottom of a **tree**, like you see in cartoons. The tree had some special branches in the form of a **garden hose**, to keep itself watered. The hose had become knotted at one end; it had got itself into a tangle playing games with a **joystick**.

What a load of nonsense, you are probably thinking, but if you take a few moments to memorise the story and visualise the events as I did, you should be able to recall the list in word-perfect order. What's more, you will probably remember the story next week and next month!

The Link Method is probably the most basic memory technique, and is very easy to understand and use. It is, however, one of the most unreliable systems, given that it relies on the user remembering the sequences of events in a story, or a sequence of images.

∞

4. The Peg Method

One concurrent theme running through all the methods is the visualisation and imagery, which helps in associating the objects with each other. As with the earlier methods of mnemonics and link, the peg system also leans heavily on the power of visualisation. The main difference between the link system and the peg system is that the Link is used to remember anything in sequence, while the Peg system is useful to memorise things in whichever order you want. This method is extremely useful for remembering telephone numbers, long digit numbers and addresses. In fact it is very useful in remembering anything which has numbers in it.

Pegs are those powerful hooks on which we hang the information. This system was first thought about by Stanislaus Mink von Wennshein in 1648 but was later improved and modified by Dr. Richard Grey. Since then, a whole lot of changes have been made by experts to make this method useful and simple.

Within the Peg Method are simple derivations, which can be used according to your own choice. However, Pegging is a difficult method to master and requires a lot of practice.

1. The Number/Rhyme System

The Number/Rhyme technique is a very simple way of remembering lists of items in a specific order. It is an example of a peg system i.e. a system whereby facts are 'pegged' to known sequences of cues (here the numbers 1 - 10). This ensures that no facts are forgotten (because gaps in information are immediately obvious), and that the starting images of the mnemonic visualisations are well known.

At a simple level it can be used to remember things such as a list of Mogul Emperors or the names of Indian Prime Ministers in their precise order. At a more advanced level it can even be used to code lists of experiments to be recalled in a science exam.

How to use the Number/Rhyme Technique

Most of us have learnt the nursery rhyme – "One, two, buckle my shoe, three, four, shut the door....." This nursery rhyme was so easy to memorise, even as a small child, because the numbers rhymed so well with the objects. The number/rhyme technique works on the same formula.

This technique works by helping you to build up pictures in your mind, in which the numbers are represented by things that rhyme with the number, and are linked to images that represent the things to be remembered.

Let me see if I can make it simpler.

Here it is:

Purpose

Obviously our purpose is to remember a list of 10 unconnected or unrelated items, and to be able to recall them on demand in any order or out of sequence, at some time in the future. It is as useful as an instant notepad for a shopping list!

How it works

It works by associating some new item - the item to be remembered - with something that you already know very well. For this to work, it is essential that you have a framework in place to which you can make the associations.

Method

1. Build the framework

By using the following table, you can set up the permanent reference points that you will be using when you make the associations.

The table lists the numbers 1 to 10, and a word that rhymes with each number, together with a suggested image. Please commit the rhymes to memory and create a mental picture of each item using your mind's eye. **Please do not proceed further through the exercise until you are sure that you have done this.** I have deliberately not shown any images, nor given suggestions, as it is your own image that must be used.

Number	Item
One	Bun
Two	Shoe
Three	Tree
Four	Door
Five	Hive
Six	Sticks
Seven	Heaven
Eight	Gate
Nine	Wine
Ten	Hen

2. Check that your pegs are secure

Are you certain that you can recall a word and your image for each number, and vice versa?

Here is a quick self-test. Ask yourself the question, and then write the answer. Check back and compare the answers from the book after you have finished. Keep practising till you have mastered the ten pegs.

Self-test

What is peg 5?
What is heaven?
What are sticks?
What is peg 9?

Your answers

Peg 5 is hive
Heaven is for number seven
Sticks are for number six
Peg 9 is wine

3. Test the method by using a set of random objects

Here is a list of 10 objects that I thought of at random today. When I was doing this, I was aware that readers might think that I had chosen these words deliberately. But this is not the case. In fact it shows that the reader is already getting into the habit of making visual images.

Item to Remember	Your Familiar Pegs
Football	Bun
Salt	Shoe
Dolphin	Tree
Statue of Liberty	Door
Telephone	Hive
Clock	Sticks
Bridge	Heaven
Moon	Gate
Carpet	Wine
Newspaper	Hen

What Next?

Make the connections

Take a minute or so to visualise the new item to be remembered interacting with your familiar peg item. Don't just think of it; actually picture the new object with your familiar object.

I find that making the picture appear funny or outrageous creates the best mental images.

Perhaps use a cartoon-style to exaggerate one or more features of the object.

Don't move on to the next item in the list until that image is firmly fixed.

To begin with, I thought of a bun containing a traditional black and white football as a filling! Crazy, I know, but it works to form a mental image. For salt, I imagined a shoe filled to the brim with salt, so much salt that it was overflowing.

Now make your own pictures, and remember to make them big, funny, silly etc.

Does it work?

To see if you created good images, why not try another self-test?

Self Test 2

List of remembered items

What was item 3?

What item number was the moon?

What was item 10?

What item number was the clock?

What was item 5?

Now Check your Answers

Item 3 was dolphin (Hopefully you pictured a dolphin with a tree!)

The moon was item 8 (Hopefully you pictured the moon with a gate).

Item 10 was newspaper (Did you remember to visualise the newspaper with a hen).

The clock was item number 6 (Clock with sticks).

Item 5 was telephone (Telephone with hive).

Are you impressed with your ability? I was, when I first tried this out.

Well done!

The amazing thing is that if you have created good images, you will still remember them a week or a month from now. In fact, they will probably stay put until you have to use the system again!

A Self-Test

Here is a tougher exercise; try it out to see whether you have made the right kind of progress.

Can you memorise the names of the ten Greek Philosophers in the right order? OK, let me tell you the names to help you out. The names of the Greek Philosophers are – Parmenides, Heraclitus, Empedocles, Democritus, Protagoras, Socrates, Plato, Aristotle, Zeno, and Epicurus.

If you have succeeded in your attempts, you have done well! For those of you who couldn't succeed, don't get disheartened! Here are the answers. Try out some more lists for practice.

A list of ten Greek philosophers could be remembered as:

1. **Parmenides** – A **BUN** topped with melting yellow **PARME**san cheese.
2. **Heraclitus** – A **SHOE** worn by **HERACL**es (Greek Hercules) glowing with a bright **Ligh T**.
3. **Empedocles** – A **TREE** from which the **M**-shaped McDonalds arches hang hooking up a bicycle **PED**al.

4. **Democritus** – Think of going through a **DOOR** to vote in a **DEMOCRaTic** election.
5. **Protagoras** – A bee **HIVE** being positively punched through (**GOR**ed?) by an atomic **PROT**on.
6. **Socrates** – **STICKS** falling onto a **SOC**k (with a foot inside!) from a **CRAT**e.
7. **Plato** – A **PLAT**e with angel's wings flapping around a white cloud.
8. **Aristotle** – Through the **GATE** bedecked with flowers, your friend called h**ARRY** is flying, clutching a b**OTtLE** of milk possessively.
9. **Zeno** – A **WINE** bottle with a **LINE** of **ZEN** buddhists meditating inside it.
10. **Epicurus** – A **HEN**'s egg being mixed into an **EPI**leptics's **CUR**e.

Try either visualising these images as suggested, or if you do not like them, come up with images of your own.

Once you have done this, try writing down the names of the philosophers on a piece of paper. You should be able to do this by thinking of the number as denoted by the first part of the sentence, then the part of the image associated with the number, then the whole image, and finally then decode the image to give you the name of the philosopher. If the mnemonic has worked, you can not only recall the names of all the philosophers in the correct order, but can also be able to spot where you have left philosophers out of the sequence. Try it - it's easier than it sounds.

Applying the Number/Rhyme Technique

You can use a peg system like this as a basis for knowledge in an entire area: the example above could be a basis for a knowledge of ancient philosophy, as images representing the projects, systems and theories of each philosopher can now be associated with the images representing the philosophers' names.

The sillier the image, the more effectively you will remember it.

2. The Number/Shape System

The Number/Shape system is very similar to the Number/Rhyme system. As with the Number/Rhyme system it is a very simple and effective way of remembering lists of items in a specific order. It is another example of the peg system.

How to use the Number/Shape Technique

This technique works by helping you to build up pictures in your mind, in which the numbers are represented by images shaped like the numbers, and are part of a compound image that also codes the thing to be remembered.

One image scheme is shown below:

1. Candle, spear, stick
2. Swan (beak, curved neck, body)
3. (rotate shape through 90 degrees!)
4. Sail of a yacht
5. A hook, sea-horse facing right
6. A golf club
7. A cliff edge
8. An hourglass
9. A balloon with a string attached, flying freely
10. A hole

If you find that these images do not attract you or stick in your mind, then change them for something, which is more meaningful to you.

As with the Number/Rhyme scheme, these images should be linked to images representing the things to be remembered.

We will use a list of more modern thinkers to illustrate the number/shape system:

1. **Spinoza** – a large **CANDLE** wrapped around someone's **SPIN**e.
2. **Locke** – a **SWAN** trying to pick a **LOCK** with its wings
3. **Hume** – a **HUM**an child engaged in **BREAST** feeding.
4. **Berkeley** – a **SAIL** on the top of a large hooked and spiked **BURR** in the **LEE** of a cliff.
5. **Kant** – a **CAN** of sausages hanging from a **HOOK**.

6. **Rousseau** – a kanga**ROO SEW**ing with a **GOLF CLUB**
7. **Hegel** – a crooked trader about to be pushed over a **CLIFF**, **HaGgL**ing to avoid being hurt.
8. **Kierkegaard** – a large **HOUR GLASS** containing captain **KIRK** and a Gu**ARD** from the starship enterprise, as time runs out.
9. **Darwin** – a **BALLOON** floating upwards, being blown f**AR** by the **WIN**d.
10. **Marx** – a **HOLE** with white chalk **MAR**ks around its edge.

Try either visualising these images as suggested, or if you do not like them, come up with images of your own.

In some cases these images may be more vivid than those in the number/rhyme scheme, and in other cases you may find the number/rhyme scheme more memorable. There is no reason why you could not mix the most vivid images of each scheme together into your own compound scheme.

The Number/Shape technique is a very effective method of remembering lists. Used in conjunction with the Number/Rhyme system it can be a powerful technique to generate potent images that can help to make well-coded mnemonics extremely effective.

The Alphabet Technique

The Alphabet system is a peg memory technique similar to, but more sophisticated than the Number/Rhyme system. At its most basic level (i.e. without the use of mnemonic multipliers) it is a good method for remembering long lists of items in a specific order in such a way that missing items can be detected. It is slightly more difficult to learn than the Number based techniques.

I would recommend that you do not attempt to learn it till you have mastered the first two techniques.

How to use the Alphabet Technique

This technique works by associating images representing and cued by letters of the alphabet with images representing the items to be remembered.

The selection of images representing letters is not based on the starting character of the name. Images are selected phonetically, i.e. in such a way that the sound of the first syllable of the image word is the name of the letter, e.g. we could represent the letter 'k' with the word 'cake'.

It is best to select the strongest image that comes to mind and stick with it.

One image scheme is given below:

A – Ace of spades
B – Bee
C – Sea
D – Dinghy
E – Eagle
F – Fan
G – Jeans
H – Hen
I – Eye
J – Jail
K – Cake
L – Elbow
M – Empty
N – Entrance
O – Oboe
P – Pea
Q – Queue
R – Ark
S – Eskimo
T – Teapot
U – Unicycle
V – Vehicle
W – WC
X – X-Ray
Y – Wire
Z – Zulu

If you find that these images do not attract you or stick in your mind, then change them for something more meaningful to you.

Once firmly visualised and linked to their root letters, these images can then be linked to the things to be remembered.

Continuing our mnemonic example of the names of philosophers, we will use the example of remembering a list of contemporary thinkers:

A – Ace - **Freud** - a crisp **ACE** being pulled out of a **FR**ying pan (**FRiED**).

B – Bee - **Chomsky** - a **BEE** stinging a **CHiM**p and flying off into the **SKY**.

C – Sea - **Genette** - a **GEN**erator being lifted in a **NET** out of the **SEA**.

D – Drum - **Derrida** - a Da**R**ing **RID**er surfing on the top of a **DINGHY**.

E – Eagle - **Foucault** - Bruce Lee fighting off an attacking **EAGLE** with Kung **FU**.

F – Fan - **Joyce** - environmentalists **JOY**fully studying a plant by hanging on the blades of a **F**an.

G – Jeans - **Nietzsche** - a pair of **JEANS** with a k**NE**e showing through the hole.

H – Hen - **Kafka** - a grand **CAF**e being blown up by a cackling **HEN**.

Try either visualising these images as suggested, or if you do not like them, come up with images of your own. Although the images are quite laboured, they are good enough to give the cues for the names being coded.

The Alphabet System is the most complex and difficult of the peg systems. It requires a longer preparation period and is more difficult to code than either the Number/Rhyme System or the Number/Shape system. It is, however, more powerful in that it allows you to code and remember a list of up to 26 items before you have to start using Mnemonic Multipliers. You may, yourself see that it is more effective to use a simpler peg system with multipliers than to use the Alphabet System without them: that is your choice.

The Journey System

The journey method is a powerful, flexible and effective mnemonic based on the idea of remembering landmarks along a well-known journey. In many ways it combines the narrative flow of the Link

Method and the structure and order of the Peg Systems into one highly effective mnemonic.

How to Use the Journey System

Purpose:

The purpose of the Journey System is to remember a list of 10 items or people, and to be able to recall them in exactly the same order without hesitation in the future. This method is specially useful if you have to introduce guests in a special order, or have to remember 10 very similar connected items in a specific order.

How it works:

It works by utilising your own familiar route through a building, or a journey that you know extremely well. Along this route, you place the objects to be remembered.

Method:

Step 1 – What is your familiar route?

You need a familiar route, or routine, that never varies, such as the route you take through your home, or the route you take to work, or the route from the main door at your office to your desk.

Step 2 – Picture yourself taking that route

In my case, I use a route through my home:

- Entering through the back door into the kitchen
- Step into the dining room
- Move into the lounge
- Into the hall
- Up the stairs
- Onto the landing
- Checking the bathroom
- Enter back bedroom
- Enter middle bedroom
- Enter front bedroom
- Visualize yourself taking that so familiar route again and again, until it is automatic.

When you are certain that your own route is pictured firmly in your mind, try the next step.

48

Step 3 – Placing the items

- Place the first item of your list at the first location of your route.
- Physically SEE the item at this location. Form that mental image.
- Progress along your route, placing each subsequent item in turn.

Step 4 – Retrace the route, recalling the items

Simply follow your route, and recall!

Step 5 – An example

- Imagine that the following fictitious list of people is to be remembered in exactly this order:

  Mayor, Policeman, Bishop, Nurse, President, King, Doctor, Soldier, Scientist, Princess.
- Place the Mayor in the first location, form a picture of him in the kitchen, don't move on until that image is firmly pictured.
- Then the Policeman in the dining room, picture the image, make sure it has registered before moving on.
- Continue with each item in the list, making sure that each visualisation is firmly fixed.

When you have finished, walk along your familiar route in your mind's eye, and recall your list of people!

The journey method is based on using landmarks on a journey that you know well.

This journey could, for example, be your journey to work in the morning, the route you use to get to the front door when you get up in the morning, the route to visit your parents, or a tour around a holiday destination. It could even be a journey around the levels of a computer game. Once you are familiar with the technique you may be able to create imaginary journeys that fix in your mind, and apply them.

Preparing the Route

To use this technique most effectively, it is often better to prepare the journey beforehand so that the landmarks are clear in your mind before you try to commit information to them. One way of doing this is to write down all the landmarks that you can recall, in order, on a piece of paper. This allows you to fix these landmarks as the significant ones to be used in your mnemonic, separating them from others that you may notice as you get to know the route even better.

You can consider these landmarks as stops on the route. To remember a list of items, whether these are people, experiments, events or objects, all you need to do is to associate these things or representations of these things with the stops on your journey.

Exercise

I may want to remember something mundane like a shopping list:

Coffee, salad, vegetables, bread, aluminium foil, fish, chicken, eggs, fruit, detergent powder.

I may choose to associate this with my journey to the supermarket. My mnemonic images therefore appear as:

1. Front door: a giant coffee percolator sitting on the doormat.
2. Rose bush in front garden: growing lettuce leaves and tomatoes around the roses.
3. Car: with potatoes, onions and cauliflower on the driver's seat.
4. End of the road: an arch of bread over the road.
5. Past garage: with sign wrapped in aluminium foil.
6. Under railway bridge: from which prawns and mackerels are dangling by their tails.
7. Traffic lights: chickens squawking and flapping on top of lights.
8. Past the post office: in front of which a hen is doing karate, with eggs heaped around it.
9. Past the primary school: with apples and oranges littered all over the school ground.
10. Supermarket car park: a filthy bucket full of dirty clothes is parked in the space next to my car!

Extending the Technique

This is an extremely effective method of remembering long lists of information: on a sufficiently long journey you could, for example,

50

remember elements on the periodic table, lists of Kings and Presidents, geographical information, or the order of cards in a shuffled pack of cards.

The system is extremely flexible also: all you need to do to remember many items is to recall a longer journey with more landmarks. To remember a short list, only use part of the route!

Long and Short Term Memory

You can use the journey technique to remember information both in the short term memory and long term memory. Where you need to use information only for a short time, keep a particular route (or routes) in your mind specifically for this purpose. When you use the route, overwrite the previous images with the new images that you want to remember. To symbolise that the list is complete, imagine that the route is blocked with cones, a 'road closed/road out' sign, or something likewise.

To retain information in long-term memory, reserve a journey for that specific information only. Occasionally travel on it in your mind, refreshing the images of the items on it.

One advantage of this technique is that you can use it to work both backwards and forwards, and start anywhere within the route to retrieve information.

Using the Journey System with other Mnemonics

This technique can be used in conjunction with other mnemonics, either by building complex coding images at the stops on a journey, linking to other mnemonics at the stops, moving onto other journeys where they may cross over. Alternatively, you may use a peg system to organise lists of journeys, etc.

The journey method is a powerful and effective method of remembering lists of information, whether short or long, by imagining images and events at stops on a journey.

As the journeys used are distinct in location and form, one list remembered using this technique is easy to distinguish from the other lists.

Some investment in preparing journeys clearly in your mind is needed to use this technique. This investment is, however, paid off many times over by the application of the technique.

In Brief

Remembering lists of information are what many of the mnemonics described in this section are all about. Almost any information can be coded into these mnemonic lists - all that is needed is the imagination in order to come up with the relevant associations.

The best techniques that can be used to remember particular lists are:

For Remembering Short Lists You Can Use:
- The Link Method
- Number/Rhyme Method
- Number/Shape Method

For Remembering Longer Lists You Can Use:
- The Journey Method

Hints on Memory Techniques

Here are a few general hints on the use of memory systems:

1. One-way or Two-way Links

Bear in mind that in some cases you may want the link to work both ways - for example if you are using a peg system (e.g. number/rhyme) to link 2 to Henry VIII, you may not want to always link Henry VIII with the number 2 (i.e. the opposite way across the link).

If, however, you are linking the French word 'chien' with the English word 'dog', you will want to ensure that the link runs in the opposite direction - i.e. that the English word 'dog' links with the French word 'chien'.

2. Remember to use Location to Separate Similar Mnemonics

By setting an application of a memory system in one location and clearly using that location as a background, you can easily separate it from a different application of the same memory system set in a different place.

3. Why Mnemonics Might Fail

Typically you may forget things that you have coded with mnemonics if the images are not vivid enough, or if the images you are using do not have enough meaning or strength for you to feel comfortable with. Try changing the images used to more potent ones.

4. Retrieving Lost Information

You may find that you need to remember information that has either been lost because part of a mnemonic was not properly coded, or that simply was not placed into a mnemonic. To try to recall the information, try the following approaches:

- In your mind run through the period when you encoded the information, carried out the action, or viewed the thing to be remembered. Reconstructing events like this might trigger associations that help you to retrieve the information.
- If the lost information was part of a list, review the other items in the list. These may be linked in some way to the forgotten item, or even if unlinked, their positions in the list may offer a different cue to retrieve the information.
- If you have any information such as general shape or purpose, try to reconstruct the information from this.

If all the above have failed, take your mind off the subject and concentrate on something else completely. Often the answer will just 'pop into your mind', as your subconscious has worked away on retrieving the information, or something you have been working on sparks an association.

∞

5. Remembering Names

Most of us 'forget' names because we never make an honest effort to remember them in the first place. In a majority of cases, you never even hear the name in the first place! Usually, when you are introduced to someone new, you hear a mumble instead of a name. Then you are either too embarrassed, or just don't care enough to ask to have it repeated.

A person's name is his most prized possession; therefore most people love to hear their own names. There is no need to be embarrassed to say you didn't hear it, and to ask to have it repeated. As a matter of fact you will flatter people when you do this.

Remembering names requires a slightly different approach to all the others explained so far in previous chapters. However, it is relatively simple when approached in a positive frame of mind. To simplify the process, you can use the following techniques.

1. Make the Association

Examine a person's face discreetly when you are introduced. Try to find an unusual feature, like ears, hairline, forehead, eyebrows, eyes, nose, mouth, chin, complexion, etc.

Create an association between that characteristic, the face, and the name in your mind. You may associate the person either with someone you know with the same name, or with a rhyme or image of the person's face or defining feature.

For instance, when I was introduced with a lady whose name was Meenakshi, I immediately connected her with the film star, Meenakshi Seshadri, thus forming an association between the two. I also noticed that she had bushy eyebrows, so I coined a phrase for her –"Bushy browed Meenakshi Seshadri". This helped me recognise her immediately, the next time I met her. I also recalled her name without any trouble.

For example, a man called Mark might have a mark/mole on his face.

A girl called Naina might have a beautiful pair of eyes.

A lad called Gautam might have a Buddha like countenance.

Someone called Renu might look like some other Renu you know.

You may come across a Jane who might be plain.

2. Enforce the Association

As you start talking to your new contact, listen to what he/she is saying about his/her job or hobbies, to make further associations between face and name.

Examples
- Renu might like to run (Renu Run).
- Prasoon might like gardening (Prasoon Flowers).
- Cathy might like cats (Catty Cathy).

3. Repetition

When you are introduced, ask for the name to be repeated. Use the name yourself as often as possible (without overdoing it!). If it is unusual, ask how it is spelled, or where it comes from, and if appropriate, exchange cards - the more often you hear and see the name, the more likely it is to sink in.

Also, after you have left that person's company, review the name in your mind several times. If you are particularly keen, you might decide to make notes.

The methods suggested for remembering names are fairly simple and obvious, but are quite powerful. Association either with images of a name or with other people can really help recall of names. Repetition and review help it to sink in.

An important thing to stress is practice, patience, and gradual improvement in remembering names.

Once you get the hang of it, making connections between people's names, faces, jobs and hobbies can be great fun.

It adds a whole new dimension to meeting people for the first time.

Here are four simple rules to apply whenever you meet someone new:

- The first rule: Be attentive when you are being introduced so that you hear the name in the first place. After you've heard the name – if you are not sure of the spelling or the pronunciation, try to spell it. Either you'll spell it correctly and flatter the person, or he'll correct you and be flattered by your interest. Either way, you've helped to 'knock' that name into your memory.

- The second rule: If you are not sure of the spelling (or even if you are), try to spell it, or have the person spell it for you. If there is any odd fact about that name, or if it is similar to a name you know, a friend's or relative's or if you've never heard a name like it before, mention it. One or two remarks about the name are a little more help in driving it into your memory.

- The third rule: Use the name as often as you can and repeat the name as often as you can during your initial conversation.

- The fourth rule: Always use the name when you say good-bye. That should help you in remembering the name till you meet the person the next time.

There are two well-established strategies for remembering people's names. The simplest basically involves paying attention. Most of the time our memory for someone's name fails because we never created an effective memory code for it.

It is an easy strategy for improving your memory for names. We can dramatically improve our memory for names simply by:

1. Paying attention to the information elaborating the information (e.g., "Barot? Is that with two t's?"; "Roy? Any relation to the writer, Arundhati Roy?", "Bjorg? What nationality is that?").

2. Repeating the information at appropriate times.

What Research Tells Us

Specific physical features (such as size of nose) are of less value in helping us remember a person than more global physical features (such as heaviness) or personality judgments (such as friendliness, confidence, intelligence). Rather than concentrating on specific features, we'd be better occupied in asking ourselves this sort of question: "Would I buy a used car from this person?" However, searching for a distinctive feature (as opposed to answering a question about a specific feature, such as "does he have a big nose?") is as effective as making a personality judgment. It seems clear that it is the thinking that is so important. To remember better, think about what you want to remember. Specifically, make a judgment ("she looks like a lawyer"), or a connection ("she's got a nose like Barbara Streisand"). The connection can be a visual image, as in the face-name association strategy.

Remembering Numbers

Day by day our lives are becoming more and more complicated. No matter what, one has to remember at least a few bank account numbers, telephone numbers etc.

How does one remember numbers?

Using mnemonic systems, remembering numbers becomes extremely simple.

There are a number of approaches, depending on the types of numbers being remembered:

1. Short Numbers

These can be stored in a number of ways:

The easiest is to use simple Number/Rhyme method associated in a story.

A simple peg system can be used, associating numbers from the Number/Rhyme method, organised with the Alphabet system.

2. Long Numbers (e.g. Pi)

This can be remembered using the Journey System. At a simple level, numbers can be stored at each stop on the journey using e.g. the Number/Shape system.

Using all the simple techniques in concert, there is no reason why you should not be able to store a 100-digit number with relatively little effort. Using the more powerful systems, holding it to 1000 digits might not be too much of a challenge.

Remembering Telephone Numbers

These can be remembered simply by associating numbers from e.g. the Number/ Rhyme system with positions in a peg system such as the Alphabet System, or the Journey System, and by further associating these with the face or name of the person whose number is being remembered.

For example, to remember that Kanta's phone number is 6353452, I can imagine myself travelling to her flat: with my destination firmly in mind, I envisage the following stops on my journey:

1. **Front door:** The door has hundreds of sticks (6) lying in front of it.
2. **Rose bush:** A small sapling (tree, 3) is growing its way through the middle of the bush.
3. **Car:** Some bees have started to build a hive (5) under the wheel of my car. I have to move it very carefully to avoid damaging it.
4. **End of road:** A tree (3) has fallen on the road. I have to drive around it.
5. **Past garage:** Someone has nailed a sign on the door (4) Strange!
6. **Under railway bridge:** The bees are building another hive (5) between the girders here.
7. **Past the municipal park:** All the trees in the park have shoes (2) hanging from their branches.

Remembering Intentions

Experts have categorised the remembering of intentions under 'Planning Memory'. Planning memory is nothing but an exercise, which helps you recall your intentions i.e. what you need to do.

Planning memory contains your plans and goals (such as, "I must pick up the dry-cleaning today"; "I intend to finish this project within three months"). Forgetting an appointment or a promise is one of the memory problems people get most upset about.

Remembering intentions is more difficult than remembering past events. It's the lack of cues to remembering that makes remembering intentions so difficult. That is why using physical objects to cue our remembering is so common. To remember intentions without relying on physical reminders, it's best to concentrate on working out an event or time that will trigger your remembering.

Set your mind to remember the link between the trigger and the intention, not the intention alone.

Why Remembering to do Things is so Difficult

Remembering intentions is in fact much more difficult than remembering events that have happened, and the primary reason is the lack of retrieval cues. This is why, of all memory tasks, remembering to do things relies most heavily on external memory aids. Reminder notes, calendars, diaries, watch-alarms, oven-timers, leaving objects in conspicuous places — all these external aids act as cues to memory.

In partial compensation for the lack of effective retrieval cues, planning memories are more easily triggered by minor cues. Even a small and seemingly insignificant thing can act as a remarkable cue. A friend of mine was reminded that her son's friend would be spending Saturday night with them when she saw an advertisement for a movie about John F. Kennedy (the child's father had the same initials: JFK). I remembered that I had to give my green dress for dry cleaning when I saw a similar green colour in the display window of a store.

How to Set Up Effective Cues

When we form an intention, we usually link it either to an event ("after we go to the swimming-pool, we'll go to the supermarket") or a time ("at 2 PM I must call Rohit"). But these triggered events or times frequently fail to remind us of our intention. This is often because the trigger is not in itself particularly distinctive. Your failure to remember to call Rohit at 2 PM, for example, may be because you paid little attention to the clock reaching that time. Or it could be because there were other competing activities triggered by that same time signal. Moreover, not all planning is linked to a triggered event or time. Quite a lot of planning simply waits upon an appropriate opportunity ("must buy some stamps sometime").

Such intentions usually need quite explicit cues. Thus, if I happened to see stamps on sale, I would probably remember my intention, but walking past, or even into, a post office, may not be enough to trigger my memory.

On the other hand, I might keep being reminded of my intention when I am in the same context as when I originally formed the intention but I am not in a position to carry it out! Hence, you get exasperated that you can never remember a particular intention when you can do something about it.

For instance, each night when I went to bed, I would remember that I had to pay my telephone bill the next day. But in the morning, it would just escape my mind and I would recall this only when I went to bed at night. The bill did not get paid for a long time because I did not remember it at the right time. Finally I kept the bill at the breakfast table, where I would not miss it – it worked!

Link the Trigger and the Intention

To deal with opportunistic planning, you should try to specify features of an appropriate opportunity. Thus, to remember to buy bread on the way home, you should think about what actions you need to take to buy the bread (for example, going through a different route) and try to form a strong link between the triggered event and your action ("today when I get to the traffic lights I'll turn left"). A reminder of your intention is less effective than being reminded of both the triggered event and the intended activity.

TIP – **Remembering the triggered event is better than trying to remember the intention alone. To remind yourself to do something, focus on the trigger, not the intent itself.**

Remembering Dates

Dates can be remembered as short number sequences as described in the 'Remembering Numbers', associated with the event to which they relate. The number of the millennium is often not needed.

Remembering Playing Cards

Once you are familiar with the Journey System, remembering the order of a pack of playing cards becomes relatively simple.

Before you try to do this, you should prepare a journey in your mind that has 54 stops. Ensure that the stops are fresh and firm in your mind.

The next step is fairly simple - what you need to do is to create an image in your mind representing each of the cards. Counting an ace as 1, and the 10 as zero, you can create a picture in your mind of an image from the Number/Shape system for the numbers Ace - 10. For the jack, queen and king, the images on the playing card are ready-made mnemonic images. The suits similarly can be represented by the suit symbols.

For example, the card representing 2 of hearts can be symbolised by a white swan with a red heart painted on its side. The ten of spades could be a hole with the handle of a spade sticking out.

It is a good idea to prepare all the images to be used beforehand, as remembering cards during a card game will have to be done quite rapidly.

As cards come up, associate the card images with the stops on your journey.

Easy!

Role of Imagery in Mnemonics

- Images are effective to the extent that they link information.
- Images are not inherently superior to words and bizarre images are not necessarily recalled better than common images.
- Imagery is chiefly effective when used with an organizing structure.
- Most mnemonic strategies are based on imagery.
- There is no doubt that imagery can be an effective tool, but there is nothing particularly special about imagery. The advantage of imagery is that it provides an easy way of connecting information that is not otherwise readily connected. However, providing verbal links can be equally effective.
- The critical element is that words or images provide a context, which links the information. Thus, imagery is only effective when it is an interactive image — one that ties together one bit of information with another.

- Visual imagery on its own is of limited value without an organizing structure, such as the method of loci or the peg word method.
- It is usually emphasized that bizarre images are remembered much better, but there is no evidence for this. In many studies indeed, ordinary images are remembered slightly well. One of the problems is that people usually find it harder to create bizarre images. Unless you have a natural talent for thinking up bizarre images, it is probably not worth bothering about.

How to Make the Techniques Work for You?

Practise, practise, practise

Practice is the key to mastering a skill. One of the critical aspects is assuredly the fact that, with practice, the demands on your attention get smaller and smaller. Interestingly, there appears to be no mental limit to the improvement you gain from practice. Your physical condition limits how much improvement you can make to a practical skill (although, in practice, few people probably ever approach these limits), but a cognitive skill will continue to improve as long as you keep practising. One long-ago researcher had two people perform 10,000 mental addition problems, and they kept on increasing their speed to the end.

How to get the most out of your practice

While practice is the key, there are some actions we can take to ensure we get the most value out of our practice:
- Learn from specific examples rather than abstract rules.
- Provide feedback while the action is active in memory (i.e., immediately). Try again while the feedback is active in memory.
- Practise a skill with subtle variations (such as varying the force of your pitch, or the distance you are throwing) rather than trying to repeat your action exactly.
- Space your practice (maths textbooks, for example, tend to put similar exercises together, but in fact they would be better spaced out).

- Allow for interference with similar skills: if a new skill contains steps that are antagonistic to steps contained in an already mastered skill, the new skill will be much harder to learn (e.g., when I changed keyboards, the buttons for page up, page down, insert, etc, had been put in a different order — the conflict between the old habit and the new pattern made learning the new pattern harder than it would have been if I had never had a keyboard before). The existing skill may also be badly affected.
- If a skill can be broken down into independent sub-skills, break it down into its components and learn them separately, but if components are dependent, learn the skill as a whole (e.g., computer programming can be broken into independent sub-skills, but learning to play the piano is best learned as a whole).

Types of Memories

Experts have classified memory into two major kinds:
- Knowledge Memory
- Personal Memory

Knowledge Memory contains information about the world while personal memory consists of information about you.

Within knowledge memory, separate domains may exist for numbers, for music, for language, and for stories. These are all types of information, which appear to be dealt with in different ways.

Personal Memory also comprises different kinds of domain like autobiographical memory, social memory (remembering names and faces of people), skill memory and planning memory.

- Autobiographical memory contains information about yourself, and about personal experiences.
- Emotions, the "facts" that describe you and make you unique, the facts of your life, and the experiences you have had, are all contained in separate domains, and processed differently.
- Your memory for emotions can help you modify your moods.

- Specific events you have experienced are only memorable to the extent that they include details special to that specific occasion.

Most events in our lives are routine, and are merged in memory into one generic memory containing the common elements of the experience.

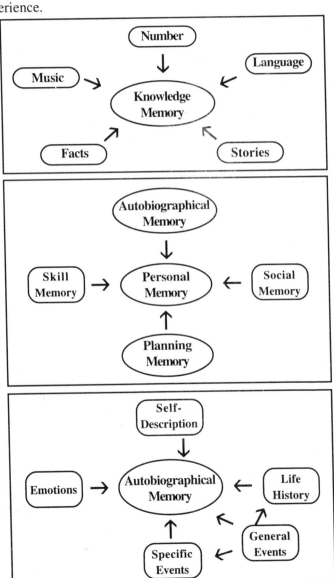

Recalling Specific Events

Event memory is usually entered via the general-event level, although the information we are searching for is usually at the specific-event level. Thus, if you're trying to retrieve the memory of going to see the movie, 'Titanic', you will probably start by accessing the general event—"going to the pictures".

Specific events over time become merged into a general event —all the times you've been to the dentist, for example, have blurred into a generic "script", which encapsulates the key experiences and actions that are typical of the going-to-the-dentist event. After the specific event has become consolidated into the script, only distinctive events are likely to be specifically remembered. That is, events when something unusual/interesting/humorous happened.

The power of these scripts is such that people often "remember" details of a specific event that never happened, merely because they are typical of the script for that event.

Our memory for events reflects what we expect to happen.

It is perhaps because of this that unexpected events and new events (first-time experiences) are better remembered. If you don't have an existing script for the event, or if the event is unusual enough not to easily fit in an existing script, then you can't mould the experience to your expectations.

The more distinctive an event - the more the event differs from your script for that type of event - the better your memory for that particular event will be. (Failures to remember trivial events, such as where you've put something, or whether you've done something, are reflections of the fact that we pay little attention to routine actions that are, as it were, already scripted).

TIP – We tend to remember the unusual and forget the common experiences. To remember an event you should look for distinctive details.

What Makes a Good Cue for Remembering Events?

One of the most interesting areas of research in the study of event memory is a small set of diary studies. In one such study, a Dutch psychologist, Willem Wagenaar, recorded his day's events everyday for six years, noting down:

- Who was involved?
- What the event was?
- Where it occurred?
- When it occurred?

Wagenaar was hoping to discover which of these different bits of information were the best retrieval cues. At the conclusion of his study he reported that 'what' was the best cue, followed by 'who' and 'where'. 'When' was the least effective (have you ever tried to remember an event on the basis of its approximate date?).

There is nothing particularly special about these types of information, however. Later, Wagenaar reanalysed his data, and found that most of the difference in the memorability of these cues was due to their relative distinctiveness. Thus, the nature of the event is usually the most distinctive aspect of the event, and the people involved, and the location, are usually more distinctive bits of information than the date or time of occurrence.

TIP – **To remember a specific event, we need a key - a unique feature that allows us to readily distinguish that event from similar events.**

Common Memory Problems

The most common memory problems faced by people occur in four key areas:

1. Knowledge Memory
2. Identity or Personal Memory
3. Event Memory
4. Planning Memory

Within each of these zones of memory, there are specific details in which people have problems. Let us have a look at the type of things one forgets–

Knowledge Memory

- Remembering information you have studied
- Remembering words

- Remembering data
- Remembering visuals

Identity Memory

- Trying to put a name to a face
- Trying to put a face to a name
- Trying to remember who someone is
- Wanting to remember someone's personal details

Event Memory

- Remembering whether you've done something
- Remembering where you've put something
- Remembering when/where something happened
- Remembering important dates

Planning Memory

- Remembering to do something at a particular time
- Knowing there's something you need to remember but you can't think what it is.

Some Tips for Better Memory

Keep your Brain Well Exercised

This is the most important thing you can do to help yourself recall those long-term memories, which now seem so elusive. Our brains need to be kept in top condition and as active now as they were in the days when we were laying down those memories we seek now. Research has proved over and over again that the old adage 'use it or lose it' applies to brainpower just as much as the muscle power.

We may feel as busy as ever, and not notice that we are doing increasingly unchallenging mental tasks. We may feel that we have 'been there and done that' when it comes to challenging thinking and problem solving. It is so much easier to fall into the pattern of inactivity.

Waking up your Brain can be Fun

What about evening classes in a new subject you have never had time for previously, or crosswords, games such as chess or bridge, logic puzzles and lateral thinking games? You could study the memory process itself if it fascinates you and find out as much as you can about how your own and your friends' memories work. It is always more fun if you can share the activity you choose with others. Making new friends and remembering all their names and interests is a challenge in itself.

Try to take on activities that are diverse, new and challenging. These type of activities can shake the brain out of its complacency and wake it up completely. When it comes to learning, age is no bar. A lot of people try to excuse themselves from learning something new by saying 'I am too old to learn'. That is an absolute crap. One can activate the brain and learn something new at any age.

Store Memories Efficiently

As we saw in the section on Storage of Memories, easy retrieval depends to a very large extent on efficient storage, so it is wise to work hard on the methods outlined there in order to find out the best methods for you. A few extra minutes spent on the coding process can work wonders while recalling.

Feed your Brain the very Best Nutrients Available

To work properly brains need food and nutrients, which are ideally suited to keep them working at peak performance.

Make Attempts to Relieve Stress and Anxiety

Anxiety and too much stress are bad for retrieval of memories, besides being detrimental to awareness and storage skills. Even normal socialising can be stressful if we are trying to make a good impression, and concentrating on the impression part. It can end with losing the thread of our remarks or forgetting what we were going to say. Instead, one should try to remember the people and their names, for future reference.

∞

6. Mental Fitness

Are you one of those who believe that mental efficiency declines with age?

As a matter of fact, it doesn't. There is no age limit for exercising the brain nor do the exercises have any side effects. In fact, the more mental exercising one does, the better are the chances of keeping an active memory till a ripe old age.

First the Good News

The decline in specific mental abilities, believed to be associated with ageing such as memory loss, sluggish thinking, and blocks in problem-solving, are not inevitable, if the brain is frequently excited by new challenges. In a major study by the National Institute of Mental Health in Philadelphia, men tested at age 81 were compared with performance on the same tests they had taken at ages 75 and 70. Researchers reported that the "pattern of decline of cognitive capabilities generally associated with advanced ageing" was "neither extensive nor consistent". Other major studies on ageing over the past 25 years (Svanborg and colleagues in Sweden, Duke University, and the National Institute on Ageing) support the findings that "mental (and physical) decline with ageing is not inevitable". Yet we have all seen elderly people who unmistakably experience mental decline, as they grow older. What can be done to preserve (and enhance) mental fitness, as we grow older?

Use It or Lose It

Not surprisingly, the same advice that we follow to achieve physical fitness applies to mental fitness—"use it or lose it." Just as daily weight repetitions in the gym or jogging strengthen certain muscle groups, mental exercises will strengthen and enhance cognitive functions over time.

69

Monique Le Poncin, founder of the French National Institute for Research on the Prevention of Cerebral Ageing, has written a fascinating book called 'Brain Fitness'. By identifying the various mental abilities in the human repertoire—perception, long- and short-term memory, and visuo-spatial memory structuralization, logic, and verbal abilities—Le Poncin has "prescribed" an exercise regimen designed to strengthen those areas that tend to become weak over the lifespan. She advocates a technique of cerebral activation, which she calls "brain fitness."

How "Brain Fitness" Works

Just as physical exercise maintains body tone, strength, and endurance, mental exercising has positive conditioning effects for people of all ages. In this chapter, we will cover the essentials that constitute a "mental workout" — daily exercises for the brain.

The goal of brain fitness is to revive certain mental abilities before they slow down. In Le Poncin's own words, "Our team does not claim to work miracles. We simply develop the previously unknown fertility of land that had been lying fallow." The exercises are simple and fun to do. And, by repeating the exercises over several weeks' time, real progress can be seen in a relatively short time.

Although these exercises have been especially created for the people of advancing age, anyone can do them in order to keep the mental faculties functioning properly.

Day-By-Day Activation

Try the following exercises when travelling to and from work, during lunch hour and breaks, or while shopping and doing housework. They take only a few moments.

Combine different variations of these exercises each day. It's important to keep a record of your progress. Use a small notebook or a dated daily diary, and note especially where you seem to have problems. Then you can self-prescribe exercises in those areas where you are the weakest. Each of the following exercises is for 'Brain Fitness', and is categorized by the specific mental ability it is designed to strengthen.

Exercise your Perceptive Abilities

The goal is to exercise perception in all five senses: sight, hearing, smell, taste, and touch.

Sight – Each day, observe an object (a photograph, for example) or a person you pass on the street. Draw it (or him or her) immediately. This exercises short-term memory. At the end of the week, redraw the seven objects or persons you have observed. This exercises long-term memory.

Smell/Taste – When dining in a restaurant or at a friend's home, try to identify the ingredients in the dishes you are served. Concentrate on the subtle flavourings of herbs and spices. Ask the waiter or your host to verify your perceptions.

Try to memorize the dishes offered on your favourite restaurant's menu. To make the exercise more challenging, memorize the prices as well. At the end of the day, recall as many of the dishes/prices as you can and write them down.

Hearing – On the telephone, practise recognizing callers before they identify themselves. Then memorize callers' phone numbers. At the end of the day, write down the people you have spoken with that day, as well as their phone numbers. At the end of the week, try writing down as many of these as you can.

Smell/Touch – Exercise your senses of smell and touch by trying to identify objects with your eyes closed.

Exercise your Visuo-spatial Abilities

Visuo-spatial abilities are related to the ability to make quick and accurate estimates of distances, areas, and volumes—the general proportions of things and their distribution in space.

Try the Following

When you walk into a room with a group of people in it, try to quickly determine how many are on your right and your left, as well as the left-right distribution of furniture and other objects. Observe objects—pens, for instance—and try to estimate their length and thickness.

When you have visited somewhere and then return home, try to draw a plan or map of the place you have seen. Repeat this exercise the next day and the day after.

Exercise your Structuralization Ability

Structuralization involves building a logical whole from disparate elements after close observation of the elements.

The following exercises will strengthen this ability.

Take a sentence from a magazine or newspaper. (This is a logical whole.) Try to make another sentence using the same words. Buy a jigsaw puzzle and practise fitting the pieces together as quickly as possible. Note the time it takes you to do this. Try it again a week later and note the time it takes you to do it again.

Exercise your Logic Abilities

Logic is the art of reasoning—finding an orderly sequence for disparate elements.

The following exercises/activities will awaken the inherently logical being inside you.

Don't use a list when shopping. Instead, invent a system to take the place of the list. Use memory aids, such as forming a complete word, or one that can be completed by adding a certain vowel or consonant from the first letters of the words for the things you need to buy. Or, you can classify foods into raw and cooked. Or, use any other system that works for you.

All games involve logical activities. Card games such as pinochle and bridge or board games of strategy such as chess or checkers are good choices. So are crossword puzzles, anagrams, and other word games. Avoid playing the same games all the time. Chess players might switch to Solitaire, while bridge players might play whist or hearts.

Playing the same game all the time leads to routine, which is the opposite of activation. The same cerebral circuits and neuronal regions are constantly used and everything else remains unused. Find new games and interests. Explore activities that are completely new to you and find new playing-partners for old—and new— games and activities.

Exercise your Verbal Abilities

Verbal abilities—the precise use of spoken or written words— make demands on short-term and long-term memory.

Listen to the morning news on the radio or TV. During the day, write down the main points of the news that you remember. Do the same in the evening.

Whenever you meet someone, try to come up with at least one anagram of his or her name. When you see a word—any word—quickly think of others that begin with the same two letters. Each time you come to the end of a chapter in a book you are reading, you must summarize it as briefly as possible, orally or in writing, to someone (real or imaginary) who has not read it. Do the same for the whole book when you finish it.

Creating the "Mentally Fit" Lifestyle

Le Poncin points out that doing mental exercises are not the end of mental fitness training.

She stresses the importance—especially for older people—of overcoming monotony and routine in our daily lives. Monotony generates mental (and emotional) lethargy and resignation. The antidote here is to organize your life in such a way that you become involved and open yourself to others through dialogue, interaction, and confrontation. Remember—failing memory and sluggish thinking is not inevitable cohorts of ageing. You have the ability to maximize your cognitive skills and enhance your memory in the older years.

What is Mental Fitness?

Mental fitness is your ability to concentrate, to reason, to visualise, to imagine, to make decisions, to solve problems and to think creatively. It depends greatly on how well and how often you exercise your mind.

How does One Work on Mental Fitness?

By dealing with challenging situations and by exposing our minds to fresh challenges, that require deep thinking and exercise the mental faculties, one can keep the mind fit and healthy.

People get mentally out of shape when they stop challenging their minds; this happens when they opt for habitual solutions rather than purposeful thought, or if they confine their thinking to a small range of interests. Getting mentally fit is like giving muscles to the mind.

To be at your best, you need to exercise all of your mental muscles, and only an all-round workout can give you this. In the same way that several body muscles work together to create physical movement, several mental muscles work together to create clear, purposeful thinking. There are four basic qualities that characterise a fit mind.

- Mental strength: Concentration
- Mental flexibility: Innovation and Creativity
- Mental endurance: Putting ideas into action
- Mental coordination: Precision and flair

Mental Workouts

- Channel mental energy into constructive thought.
- Improve the attention span.
- Increase concentration.
- Increase endurance.
- Improve problem-solving capability.
- Enhance the power to analyse.
- Improve decision-making ability.
- Enhance creativity.
- Create awareness.
- Increase knowledge.
- Reduce threat of mental illnesses.
- Help in goal visualisation.
- Bring harmony into life.
- Improve personal performance.

Brain Workouts

There are various ways to exercise your brain. While some exercises activate your left-brain, i.e., the analytic, logical part of your mind, others work your right brain, i.e., the intuitive, spatial part of your mind. Some help you relax, while others exercise your inner muscles with mental callisthenics, altogether working out your whole mind.

Thumb Rules for a Good Mental Workout

- Leave your concerns and problems outside, in the locker room.

74

- Intend to strengthen yourself.
- Relax your physical body. It helps to concentrate.
- Stimulate your brain.
- Create your own mental gym and then take it anywhere.
- Exercise, don't analyse.
- Take your time to explore your inner world.
- Repeat the exercises.
- Keep your mind open and ready to learn.
- Keep conditioning your mind.

Give your Mind the Right Stimulus

Breathing exercises are the right way to begin a mental workout. They relax your mind by relaxing your body. You can do Pranayam to settle into the rhythm of your breathing, and keep your body loose.

Adopt a physical posture that helps to concentrate. Find a mental rhythm that builds a momentum in your work. To become more aware of what's happening, stop what you are doing once in a while and look, listen and ask yourself, what's happening?

Look around the room and find circles, squares or rectangles. Visualise as many objects as you can in those shapes. Categorise the items in the room to fall into those shapes.

Focus your attention – Recall the events in the last 24 hours. When you have succeeded in doing so, go over the events that occurred in the past 48 hours. If you are able to recall the events, keep practising till you become proficient at the game.

Experiment and try out novel ideas. Try new things with your body. Most of us perform best with our right hand and can't use the left hand so well. Try to become ambidextrous i.e. equally adept at using both the hands. To do so, write with the non-writing hand; comb your hair with that hand. Lay down in a position you don't normally lie in. Take an impromptu break. Colour or read upside down. Switch off the light and make your way to the door. Make connections through similes, metaphors or more. Take creative risks, experiment.

Pay attention to only what you want to or have to remember; don't try to retain everything.

Use cues to remember, visualise, associate, and create a story. Look beyond assumptions; things are not always what they seem to be.

In a bus gaze at someone's head or a certain point in the vehicle for five minutes without diverting your attention. Add the digits of the front car's number on the number plate; make whole sentences of the letters, e.g. TTTL could become Turn To The Left. Solve imaginary questionnaires. Ask yourself questions starting with imaginary ideas - e.g., what if the sky was permanently red? View things or dramas as if you were a four-year-old.

- Devise stories.
- Calculate anything mentally that you can.
- Read backwards, read mirror images. Recite the national anthem backwards, your favourite song or saying or poem backwards, skip a word and recite again. Look at things upside-down; get a different perspective.
- View every individual as another entity.
- Solve a crossword.
- Unclutter your thinking by identifying what you need to think about. You can do this by jotting everything that's in your mind on a piece of paper, then rating them according to priority. This also relieves stress, as it helps you face what you are running away from.
- Find out what is important to you. Visualise and link the items on a grocery list or ideas in your mind through imaginary links or negative ideas. Open your cupboard, observe the shelf for a few minutes, close the cupboard and recollect as many things as you can. Imagine yourself as having attained your goal and life after the achievement - especially when you are down and out. Replay happy memories in your life.
- Place yourself in other people's shoes. Try and think like them, act like them. One of my favourites is imitating the walk of people I knew. I could judge their nature by it. Recollect what happened in an hour or in a day; visualise people you met, things that you did and enjoyed. Recollect the faces of your friends and colleagues.
- Visualise movies as you think you would have directed them. Diverse stimulation is the key. Get out of the rut, do something

different every day, visit a new store or friend, take up a new hobby, try a new route, change the furniture, learn a new language, etc.

- Be more aware - observe, see, hear, smell and sense all around you and replay it in your mind.
- Pay attention.
- Take a break. Unwind. Develop the skill of letting go fully by setting aside some time each day to do nothing. To keep conditioning your mind, maintain a journal, write down the exercises you did and that which worked for you. You can write anything that you want to think about. Read it whenever you seem to have a block.
- Make your own mental exercises; exercise every faculty of your brain anywhere and everywhere. Remember, everything in life is only as difficult as you think it is.
- Enhance, inspire and challenge your mind to the fullest - only you can make it perfect. Remember, the genius is in your mind.

Increasing your Brain Power

We forget information for several reasons; because we don't use the information, we confuse it with other information, we decide the information does not match what we already believe, or we never really learned the information in the first place. In order to help increase your memory and maximize your brainpower, follow these important tips:

1. *Memorize from General to the Specific.* Study the big picture, and then learn the details. This is similar to writing an outline where you note the general subject and list the details under it. It is a much more effective process of learning.

2. *Pay attention and consciously choose to remember the information needed to commit to memory.* Tell yourself, "I must remember this!", before studying or reading the material or instructions.

3. *Visualize or picture in your mind what you wish to remember.* It is easier to remember images or key words imprinted in your mind, than to try and bring back general,

non-specific lengthy texts or sequence of events. Visualize an outline or steps taken to accomplish your task and commit that to memory, instead.

4. **Make associations between the new ideas and information you wish to remember** and information, ideas, persons, things, etc. that you already know. In other words, understand the concepts and make connections that relate to each other.

5. **Over-learn by repeating information.** Seven is the magic number.

Repeat difficult information seven times a day for seven days. When you are reading, highlight headings, outlines, pertinent words or phrases and review continually. Spend only ten minutes of your time reviewing and studying. Remember, that the brain absorbs only 20 per cent of what it takes in at one time. So the shorter the study period, the more the brain will retain.

6. **Take the time to learn the material and commit it to memory.** Cramming doesn't work. It only commits the information to your short-term memory and you will forget what you never really learned in the first place.

i. *Write it down!* Then, even if you forget it, you'll be able to learn it again. Keep a pocket-sized calendar or notebook handy for making notes and jotting down thoughts you have during the day. Keep a note pad and pencil by your bed. Some of our greatest ideas come to us in the middle of the night, or as we're dropping off to sleep. Studies have shown that you remember more if you study right before you go to sleep. For some people it is in the afternoon, instead of the morning. But anytime can be the best time to learn as your brain is always taking in new information.

ii. *Read aloud the material you want to remember.* You can improve your learning and memory by as much as 40 per cent by using this simple technique.

iii. *Use different methods of memorizing things.* You should try one method for memorizing math concepts, and another for memorizing language or arts, such as poems, or the constitution.

iv. The best approach to improving your memory and maximizing your brainpower is to *use your memory as often as possible! The more you use it, the better it will get!*

Living in the Information Age

Boyd Swinburn, Medical Director of New Zealand's National Heart Foundation, while talking of the environmental determinants of behaviour, says "The problem people have with keeping weight off is not because they're weak-willed, but because our environment doesn't encourage regular exercise, and encourages unhealthy eating". In the same way, our environment encourages memory failure.

One weekday edition of the New York Times is said to contain more information than the average person in 17th century England was likely to come across in an entire lifetime. In 1971, the average American was targeted by at least 560 daily advertising messages. Twenty years later that had risen to 3000 messages a day.

In the past thirty years, the average TV news "soundbite" has decreased from around 42 seconds to some 8 seconds. The typical business manager is said to read 1 million words a week.

According to Oracle's Bill Seawick, the pace of technological change is such that people have to learn new technologies every three or four months.

Too Many Faces

Apart from the people we actually physically meet (if only in passing on the street), think of all the different faces that appear on our TV screens. Our ability to recognize faces is truly incredible, and probably better than any other memory ability, but we make very heavy demands on it today. In the old days, you would have a circle of people with whom you would spend your whole life. When you married, you would widen this circle. Maybe you emigrate, and start a new life, but earlier only a very small number of people changed their lives as constantly as people do today.

Information Overload!

We all have trouble remembering the details of specific bits of information. Too much information coming too fast encourages us to opt out — to let our minds wander and give up the unequal struggle. Information overload is implicated in increased stress, confusion, frustration, impaired judgment, decreased benevolence, and overconfidence. We tend to pass the buck more; we tend to ignore anything we can get away with ignoring; we tend to give less time to things.

Remembering Well is about Remembering Wisely

In a way, these strategies are adaptive. The trouble is that these strategies aren't thought out. We're letting the situation control what we attend to, when we should be the ones controlling what we choose to attend to.

Coping with the deluge of data requires thoughtful selection. There's nothing wrong with not remembering everything, but we should be the ones choosing what we're going to remember.

Learning is forever.

Learning new skills and new information isn't something we leave behind in school. It's something we have to keep doing forever.

External Memory Aids

What are External Memory Aids?

External memory aids are the reminding devices that we use when we are not able to optimise our memory to remember things. There are many external memory aids or devices that people use, some of them are simplistic in nature while others are quite technical in their working. One of the simplest memory aids has been used by women from centuries and that is to tie a knot in the *sari pallu* or in a handkerchief to remind them of something. Many women still use this simple device as an external memory aid.

External Memory Aids Include Such Strategies As:

- Taking notes
- Making shopping lists
- Entering appointments in a diary or on a calendar
- Writing a memo to yourself
- Writing on the back of your hand
- Taking photographs

- Using clocks, oven-timers, alarms or watches, etc
- Putting objects in a conspicuous place
- Putting a knot in your handkerchief
- Asking someone to help you remember

Making Lists

Making lists or writing reminder notes to yourself, is one of the most widespread external memory aids. It seems that list making is primarily helpful as a way of organizing (encoding) information, rather than its more obvious role in retrieving. More often than not, people do not actually use the list or note to 'remember'. The act of making it is sufficient to aid later recall.

However, there are situations where list-making appears appropriate but is not in fact the best strategy. For example, one study found that the waitresses who went from table to table to take drink orders were much better at remembering the orders if they visualized the drinks in particular locations rather than when they wrote the orders down.

It is perhaps the time pressure in that kind of situation that makes an internal strategy more effective than an external one.

When to Use Mental Strategies

When you can't rely on external prompts (e.g., acting in a play); when external prompts are difficult to prepare (e.g., because you lack writing materials), or hard to use (you have blisters in your writing hand); when you didn't expect to need to recall something, and have nothing prepared; when using external aids interferes with other behaviour (understanding what's going on, taking orders etc.); when carrying external aids would be undesirable or inconvenient (e.g., when driving); when the interval between learning and recall is very short (as when you need to remember a phone number only long enough to dial it).

When to Use External Memory Aids

When a number of interfering activities occur between encoding and recall (e.g., having to remember to buy groceries after work); when there is a long time between encoding and recall (e.g., needing to make a doctor's appointment two months in the future);

when internal aids are not trusted to be sufficiently reliable (as when precise details need to be remembered, e.g. strict timing to check a cake in the oven); when information is difficult, and doesn't cohere easily (e.g., remembering lectures); when there is insufficient time to properly encode information; when memory load is to be avoided (as when you are attending to more than one activity).

How effective are external memory aids? In general, external aids are regarded as easier to use, more accurate, and more dependable, than mental strategies. However, with the exception of note taking, there has been little research into the effectiveness of external memory aids. The most that can be said is that, by and large, people believe they can be effective (with the emphasis, perhaps, on 'can').

One problem with external aids is that most of them are highly specific in their use. Their effective use also requires good habits. It's no good remembering to make a note in your diary if you don't remember to look at it.

Facilitation vs. Memory Improvement

Memory is facilitated when actions are taken to improve memory for specific information or on a specific occasion. Memory is improved when a person masters various learning strategies and uses them as a matter of habit. What generally happens as a result of participating in a memory-improvement course is temporary memory improvement, known as facilitation of memory performance. Sometimes this is all that is desired. For example, a teacher or supervisor often tries to create conditions whereby the student's or employee's memory in the learning situation is facilitated, rather than trying to permanently improve their memory.

When a teacher or parent teaches a child the rhyme "Thirty days hath September, April, June and November...", the aim is to help the child remember a specific set of facts — the number of days in each month. This is facilitation of memory performance. If instead, the instructor had explained mnemonic strategies — what they are, how they can be used, when they are appropriate, how you can create them, etc — and then gave as an example "Thirty days ...", that would be an attempt to permanently improve memory.

The difference between memory facilitation and permanent memory improvement lies in the extent to which facilitation strategies are used. In most cases, such strategies are adopted for a particular occasion only.

For example, someone might tell you the phone number — 560-1984 — and suggest that it is easy to remember because you were born in 1956 (in 1956 you were 0) and 1984 is of course the name of George Orwell's famous book. If you generalized that strategy and began to remember all new phone numbers by transforming them into meaningful chunks, that would be memory improvement, but if, as is much more likely, you simply followed the recommendation for remembering that particular number, that would be memory facilitation.

∞

7. Memorizing Methods for Students

Mnemonic Techniques and Specific Memory

Although it can be the easiest to remember those things that you understand well, sometimes you must rely on rote memory. Mnemonic techniques are more specific memory aids. The following techniques can be used to facilitate such memorization.

1. **Acronyms** – Acronym is a method in which you form acronyms by using the first letter from a group of words to form a new word. This is particularly useful when remembering words in a specified order. Acronyms are very common in ordinary language and in many fields. Some examples of common acronyms include NBA (National Basketball Associations), SCUBA (Self Contained Underwater Breathing Apparatus), BTUs (British Thermal Units), and LASER (Light Amplification by Stimulated Emission of Radiation). What other common acronyms can you think of? The memory techniques in this section, for example, can be rearranged to form the acronym "SCRAM" (Sentences/acrostics, Chunking, Rhymes & songs, Acronyms, and Method of loci).

I have used acronyms extensively during my student years, to a very useful end result. For example, I used the acronym **BHAJSAB** to remember the important rulers from the Mughal dynasty – Babar, Humayun, Akbar, Jehangir, Shahjahan, Aurangzeb and Bahadur Shah Zafar.

Let us suppose that you have to memorize the names of four kinds of fossils for geology: 1) Actual remains, 2) Petrified, 3) Imprint, and 4) Moulds or casts. Take the first letter of each item you are trying to remember: APIM. Then, arrange the letters so that the acronym resembles a word you are familiar with: PAIM or IMAP.

Although acronyms can be very useful memory aids, they do have some disadvantages. Firstly, they are useful for rote memory, but do not aid comprehension. Be sure to differentiate between comprehension and memory, keeping in mind that understanding is often the best way to remember. Some people assume that if they can remember something, then they must "know" it, but memorization does not necessarily imply understanding. A second problem with acronyms is that they can be difficult to form; not all lists of words will lend themselves equally well to this technique. Finally, acronyms, like everything else, can be forgotten if not committed to memory.

2. **Sentences/Acrostics** – Acrostics are quite like acronyms, in the sense you use the first letter of each word you are trying to remember. Instead of making a new word, though, you use the letters to make a sentence.

Here are some examples:

My Dear Aunt Sally (mathematical order of operations: Multiply and Divide before you Add and Subtract).

King Phil Came Over for the Genes Special (Kingdom, Phylum, Class, Order, Genus, Species) can be used by the biology students to remember classification of plants and animals.

In medical college one commonly used acrostics to remember the names of the eight wrist bones is – She is too pretty, try to catch her.

Can you think of other examples? Like acronyms, acrostics can be very simple to remember and are particularly helpful when you need to remember a list in a specific order. One advantage over acronyms is that they are less limiting. If your words don't form easy-to-remember acronyms, using acrostics may be preferable. On the other hand, they can take more thought to create and require remembering a whole new sentence rather than just one word (as is the case with acronyms). Otherwise, they present the same problem as acronyms in that they aid memorization but not comprehension.

Exercise: Practise Using Acrostics

- Try making up a sentence (acrostic) to remember the five mnemonic techniques discussed in this section.
- Now come up with acrostics for the main sections of a chapter from one of your textbooks.

3. **Rhymes & Songs** – Rhythm, repetition, melody, and rhyme can all aid to memory. Are you familiar with Homer's Odyssey? If you are familiar with the book, then you know that it is quite long. That is why it is so remarkable to realize that storytellers who would rely solely on their memories would narrate this epic, along with many ancient Greek stories. The use of rhyme, rhythm, and repetition helped the storytellers remember them.

   You can use the same techniques to remember information from courses. For example, even the simple addition of familiar rhythm and melody can help. Do you remember learning the alphabet? Many children learn the letters of the alphabet to the tune of "Twinkle, Twinkle, Little Star." In fact, a student demonstrated how she memorized the quadratic formula (notorious among algebra students for being long and difficult to remember) by singing it to a familiar tune!

   Using these techniques can be fun, particularly for people who are creative. Rhymes and songs draw on your auditory memory and may be particularly useful for those who can learn tunes, songs, or poems easily. Like the other techniques in this section, however, they emphasize rote memory, not understanding. Also, when devising rhymes and songs, don't spend too much time creating them. Use these techniques judiciously and don't let them interfere with your studying.

4. **Method of Loci** – The Loci method was used by ancient Greek orators to remember their speeches. In modern parlance, it is also called the Journey Method. It combines the use of organization, visual memory, and association. Before using the technique, you must identify a common path that you walk. This can be the walk from your dorm to class, a walk around your house, whatever is familiar. What is essential is that you have a vivid visual memory of the path and objects along it. Once you have determined your path, imagine yourself walking

along it, and identify specific landmarks that you will pass. For example, the first landmark on your walk to campus could be your dorm room, next may be the front of the residence hall, next a familiar statue you pass, etc. The number of landmarks you choose will depend on the number of things you want to remember.

Once you have determined your path and visualized the landmarks, you are ready to use the path to remember your material. This is done by mentally associating each piece of information that you need to remember with one of these landmarks. For example, if you are trying to remember a list of mnemonics, you might remember the first—acronyms—by picturing SCUBA gear in your dorm room (SCUBA is an acronym).

You do not have to limit this to a path. You can use the same type of technique with just about any visual image that you can divide into specific sections. The most important thing is that you use something with which you are very familiar.

Exercise: Method of Loci

1. If someone reads a list of unrelated words to you, just once, how many do you think you could remember? Give it a try. Have someone read a list of 10 words to you at a slow but steady pace (about 1 word per second). Rather than using any of the memory techniques presented here, simply try to concentrate on the words and remember them. How many words did you remember?

2. Now take a few minutes to identify a path or object that you can use in the method of loci. Familiarize yourself with each of sections of your path or object. Mentally go through each of the loci (locations) and visualize them as best as you can. Remember, it is important to be able to visualize and recall each location readily. Once you have done this, have your friend read you a different list of words. This time, try to create visual images of the words associated with one of the locations. This may not come easy at first, but with practice you should be able to create these visual images more readily.

If you find that you are facing difficulty in coming up with the images quickly, practise on some more lists until you have improved. Chances are, when you become familiar with using this technique, you will be able to remember many more words (maybe all 10 items).

5. **Chunking** – This is a technique generally used when remembering numbers, although the idea can be used for remembering other things as well. It is based on the idea that short-term memory is limited in the number of things that can be contained. A common rule is that a person can remember 7 (plus or minus 2) "items" in short-term memory. In other words, people can remember between 5 and 9 things at one time. You may notice that local telephone numbers have 7 digits. This is convenient because it is the average amount of numbers that a person can keep in his or her mind at one time.

When you use "chunking" to remember, you decrease the number of items you are holding in memory by increasing the size of each item. In remembering the number string 64831996, you could try to remember each number individually, or you could try thinking about the string as 64 83 19 96 (creating "chunks" of numbers). This breaks the group into a smaller number of "chunks." Instead of remembering 8 individual numbers, you are remembering four larger numbers. This is particularly helpful when you form "chunks" that are meaningful or familiar to you (in this case, the last four numbers in the series are "1996", which can easily be remembered as one chunk of information).

6. **Practice Makes A Man Perfect** (or closer to it anyway) – Okay, it may not be a mnemonic, but repeating is still a great memory aid. Remember the children's game "I'm going on a picnic and I'm bringing...." As each new object is added, the old objects are repeated. People can often remember a large number of objects this way. When remembering a list of things, you might try a similar concept. Once you are able to remember 5 items on your list without looking, add a 6th, repeat the whole list from the start, add a 7th, and so on. It can be quite intimidating to see long lists, passages, or equations that you are expected to commit to memory. Break up the information into small bits that you can learn, one step at a time, and you may be surprised at how easy it can be. You might even utilize grouping techniques, like those discussed earlier, to form meaningful groups that you can learn one at a time.

Brain Gym Exercises

The brain gym exercises can be used by teachers to help students improve concentration during a class. Parents, while teaching their children at home, can also use these exercises very effectively. They are especially helpful to focus the concentration of fidgety, restless and hyperactive children.

These simple exercises are based on the work presented by Carla Hannaford, Ph.D. Carla Hannaford is a neuro-physiologist and educator with more than 28 years of teaching experience. In her best selling book "Smart Moves", Dr. Hannaford states that our bodies are very much a part of all our learning, and learning is not an isolated "brain" function. Every nerve and cell is a network contributing to our intelligence and our learning capability. Many educators have found this work quite helpful in improving overall concentration in class. Introduced here, you will find four basic "Brain Gym" exercises, which implement the ideas developed in "Smart Moves", and can be used quickly in any classroom. They are surprisingly simple, but very effective!

Drink Water

As Carla Hannaford says, "Water comprises more of the brain (with estimates of 90 per cent) than of any other organ of the body." Having students drink some water before and during class can help "grease the wheel". Drinking water is very important before any stressful situation, e.g. during class tests! It is simply because we tend to perspire under stress, and dehydration can affect our concentration negatively. The water can take care of the dehydration, and it reduces the stress and improves the concentration.

"Brain Buttons"

This exercise helps improve blood flow to the brain to "switch on" the entire brain before a lesson begins. The increased blood flow helps improve concentration skills required for reading, writing, etc.

Brain buttons

Put one hand so that there is as wide a space as possible between the thumb and index finger. Place your index and thumb into the slight indentations below the collarbone on each side of the sternum. Press lightly in a pulsing manner.

At the same time put the other hand over the navel area of the stomach. Gently press on these points for about 2 minutes.

"Cross Crawl"

This exercise helps coordinate right and left-brain by exercising the information flow between the two hemispheres. It is useful for spelling, writing, listening, reading and comprehension.

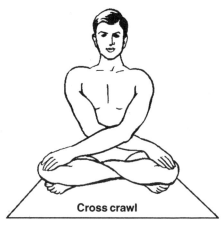

Cross crawl

You could do this exercise standing or sitting, as it suits you. Put the right hand across the body to the left knee as you raise it, and then do the same thing for the left hand on the right knee just as if you were marching. Just do this either sitting or standing for about 2 minutes.

"Hook Ups"

This works well for nerves before a test or special event such as making a speech. Any situation, which might cause nervousness, calls for a few "hook ups" to calm the mind and improve concentration.

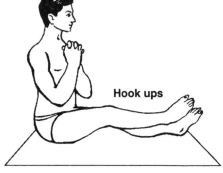

Hook ups

This can also be done either standing or sitting. *Cross the right leg over the left at the ankles.* Take your right wrist and cross it over the left wrist and link up the fingers so that the right wrist is on top. Bend the elbows out and gently turn the fingers in towards the body until they rest on the sternum (breast bone) in the centre of the chest. Stay in this position. Keep the ankles crossed and the wrists crossed and then breathe evenly in this position for a few minutes. You will be noticeably calmer after that time.

Using Music in the Classroom

Six years ago, researchers reported that people scored better on a standard IQ test after listening to Mozart. You would be surprised at how much music can also help English learners.

Using Coloured Pens

The use of coloured pens can help the right brain to remember patterns. Each time you use the pen, it reinforces the learning process. In fact, for younger children, using different colour pens to write the headlines and creating distinction between the paragraphs can be very helpful.

Helpful Drawing Hints

"A picture paints a thousand words". - Easy techniques to make quick sketches that will help any artistically challenged teacher. Use drawings on the board to encourage and stimulate class discussions.

The Modern Approach to Memory Improvement

Long before books arrived, telling stories was the only way to pass information from one person or generation to the next. Throughout history, people have sought to improve their memory for storytelling. A variety of mental techniques have been passed down over the centuries as skills for studying. Unfortunately, the old mental techniques are just about all you get from conventional books, tapes and courses.

Because the memory improvement profession has emphasized old mental techniques, most memory experts incorporated little or nothing of new methods of modern science.

For example, any mental technique won't be very effective, if a person fails to notice and remember key information during the interactions with others. The new approach to memory improvement involves taking into account various conditions of the person's physical and/or emotional condition. The new approach is, therefore, multi-modal and highly empowering.

If someone wants to improve his memory performance, in addition to learning the right ways to approach each memory skill (such as the best strategies for remembering names), attention must be paid to one's overall health and lifestyle. The new approach also helps explain why peoples' memory performance varies. People vary in their readiness to perform memory tasks because their mental, physical, and emotional states vary from week to week, day to day, and sometimes even hour to hour. Like a psychological biorhythm, a person's mental state, physical state, and emotional state change with stress, health status, standard of living, and other factors. Such state changes can have an immense effect on a person's memory.

Hundred Percent Usage of the Brain

If our species were meant to do manual tasks with one finger, we would NOT have been born with ten fingers. If we were meant to use only 10 percent of our brain cells to lead a happy life, we would not have been born with 10 times as much to use. In fact, man (Homo Sapiens) is the only creature on earth that does not use its 100 percent brain capacity.

Dolphins have about the same neuronal capacity as man, yet they live as intelligent, fun-loving and harmonious creatures with their environment. They use their complete brains, not just a fraction. Is it too much of an imaginative stretch to assume that the more you use your brain capacity, the more harmonious your life could be? Can you really imagine a 100 percent brain user engaged in crime, war, starvation, disease, prejudice or environmental destruction? Of course not!

So in other words, we're creatures that are designed just as perfectly as every other creature on earth, but we're just not using all the potential available to us like all other creatures! Why? Could it be that we no longer know HOW to connect to our "energy source" like all other creatures? Or is it that we don't care to make the free CHOICE to do so? Free will is such a confusing thing to 10 percent brain users controlled by "knee-jerk" desires of the body!

Regardless of the reason for the brain neglect, it's the 'use it or lose it' axiom at work here, because average human beings are losing over 100,000 brain cells every day due to disuse or misuse. The more a person neglects using his brain potential, the more his condition is likely to worsen! Is there any wonder why the diseases such as Alzheimer's, Dementia, Senility, Parkinson's and other brain disorders are increasing so alarmingly?

What is the solution? Can we really use 100 percent of our brains and improve the quality of our lives? Of course we can. Instead of having memory loss, we can become memory wizards. Instead of being stymied by the simplest problems, we can become creative "geniuses."

Many people get so "stuck" in daily routines and knee-jerk patterns of behaviour that they often do not see the many opportunities and alternatives around them, every day. To begin the process of stimulating your 100 percent brain, practise the following 7 brain-gymnastic drills for seven days and see for yourself the progress you can make in such a short span of time. Each drill touches upon a different area of your brain.

1. Get used to your body in new ways. Switch your handedness and comb your hair, brush your teeth, stir your coffee or do other simple tasks with your non-dominant hand. Close your eyes and "sense" your way slowly around a room. Get truly conscious of the sounds and smells in the space around you. Also, use your feet to pick up things, flush the toilet or close a door. Read a page in a book held vertically and then read it upside down!

2. Where normally you would criticize someone, find something to compliment them on instead! Suspend your judgment about that person as well, and view him (her) as simply another human being with different viewpoints than your own.

3. Look in your refrigerator briefly, but thoroughly. Then close the door and enumerate the items contained therein. Do the same with a room of your house, a display window in a shop or a detailed picture on the wall.

4. For 5 minutes every day, put yourself in another person's shoes and view things from another person's perspective for a change and see how it feels. Suspend your judgment about that person as well. Pretend you're an actor and taking on the part of that person in exact demeanour and manner. Feel how it feels!!

5. Whenever you catch yourself worrying, doubting or looking down on yourself, think instead of what you most want out of life in complete detail, and affirm to yourself the achievement of the same. Replay this positive inner movie whenever negative thoughts intrude you.

6. At the end of every hour, review what happened to you during the previous 60 minutes. This is good practice for getting more mindful throughout the day, and should only take seconds to do. At the day's end, mentally review all the events that happened to you throughout the day up to your present point. Memory gaps about your day's events reveal unconscious moments.

7. To develop flexibility and adaptability to change in your life, do something different every day. Shop at a different store. Take a different route home. Bake a pie or a loaf of bread. Involve yourself in a new game or sport, like roller-skating, bowling, karate or skydiving. Introduce yourself to a new neighbour. The sameness every day is a death knell to your brain. For more complete usage of your brain, diverse stimulation is the key. It also gets you unstuck from habits and ruts that are bringing you unfavourable results.

Some More Brain Exercises

You've lost your keys for the umpteenth time. You return home from the grocery store and realize you forgot the most important item. You open your mouth to talk but forget what you want to say? Like a pencil low on lead, our minds need sharpening. Here are some daily exercises you can do to keep the brain from getting flabby.

1. Toss the calculator. Next time you balance your cheque book, do it in your head or on paper. Add those numbers, compare balances, until the totals are correct (or as close as you'll accept). You may actually feel the numbers whizzing through your mind as you calculate.

2. After you have finished the meal at a restaurant, figure the tip in your head. Don't even use paper to determine fifteen or twenty per cent. There are some short cuts that you may use, such as making the tip equal to double the tax (depending on your area's tax rate).

3. Keep the grocery list hidden. Write the list; pack it away in your purse or pocket and head for the store. As you stroll the aisles, think about what's for dinner, who you are entertaining, whether or not you're providing scout snacks. Visualize your refrigerator and pantry to see what's in stock. Just before checking out, check your list to see if you've remembered it all.

4. Do crosswords and word jumble daily. It's a sad truth that many of these mind activities are given scant attention and even the ones that appear on your daily newspaper remain completely blank when they are so good for your brain. Make it a habit and soon you'll be in the rhythm of doing these activities every day.

5. Play board games, charades, and word games. Scrabble, Brainvita, Chinese Checkers, especially Chess are very good for exercising the brain. Any games that force you to use math and language skills are tapping into those areas of your brain that may need some stirring.

6. Learn a new word a week. Have each family member bring a new word to dinner once a week. Go over the meaning and how the new word relates to your family. Visualize the word being filed in your mind and review it from time to time. Keep track of the words.

7. Play name games with yourself when you meet new people. For example, if you meet Tarun and he is over six feet, think of the Two "T" man - Tarun and tall! Be creative in your approach. If Suchitra is an orthodontist, think of it as "Suchitra, with the Straight Teeth."

8. Recite the alphabet backwards until you are proficient. Try this exercise three times a day until you can do the backwards version as quickly as the regular version. This takes work!

9. Read riddle books and try to solve them. These also make good party icebreakers.

10. Get organized! Keep your keys in the same place each day. Clean your desk. Straighten your closet. When your life is organized, you spend less time worrying about where things are and other details that cloud the mind. Just the process of organizing will clear your mind.

11. Take up a hobby that forces you to think outside the box. Some examples include learning a foreign language, which is very different from English, such as Russian. Or learn how to read music. Or, on a practical note, enhance your computer skills by either teaching yourself a new programme, or taking a class. Make certain to incorporate the newly acquired information into your lifestyle.

12. Increase your base of knowledge. When you meet someone new, ask questions using the "who, what, where, when, why, how" formula. Ask who the person is (name), what is his or her career, where they work, when they began their career, why they enjoy that line of work, and how they decided to pursue their career. Then go deeper with questions, such as, "What does it mean to be a palaeontologist?" or "What is the most challenging part of dentistry?" Listen closely, and you will gain new knowledge. Learning is a way to continually sharpen the mind.

We exercise our bodies to keep them firm. It's important to do the same for our minds.

Special Learning Tricks for Students

Improving Learning

In the previous chapter, we have discussed memory processes and introduced you to some basic concepts of memory. What we have presented, however, is just the tip of the iceberg. If you review research on memory and learning, you will find that there exists a vast amount of information on the subject. Our purpose is to make it more personally and academically effective, and to see how this knowledge can be put into practice. In other words, how can it help you improve your memory? Thus, we focus on memory techniques and strategies.

1. **Order, Order** – Organizing and ordering information can significantly improve memory. Imagine, for example, how difficult it would be to remember a random list of 62 letters. On the other hand, it would not be difficult to memorize the first sentence in this paragraph (consisting of 62 letters).

   Similarly, learning a large amount of unconnected and unorganised information from various sources can be very challenging. By organizing and adding meaning to the material prior to learning it, you can facilitate both storage and retrieval. In other words, you can store it better and recall it easier.

The following concepts can help you pull various informations together in order to enhance understanding and organization. This can mean organizing material on paper, such as when you make an outline or idea web, or simply organizing material in your memory, such as learning it in a particular order or making intentional associations between ideas.

2. **The Funnel Approach** – This means learning general concepts before moving on to specific details. When you study a document in this manner, you focus on getting a general framework, or overview, before filling in the details. When you understand the general concepts first, the details make more sense. Rather than disconnected bits of information to memorize, such as history dates, it is easier to learn them within the overall framework.

   Seeing how the smaller details relate to one another, you process the information more deeply (which helps you store, and later retrieve it from memory). This idea is probably familiar—there are many learning strategies based on the funnel approach. For example, the approach is used in previewing a chapter for the major ideas as a way to enhance your comprehension of details contained in the chapter. You may also notice that many textbook chapters are organized in a "general to specific" format. Finally, you probably use this type of approach when studying from an outline, matrix, or concept map. Because of their organization, these tools are particularly well-suited for learning from general to specific.

3. **Organising Through Meaning and Association** – We have already discussed the concept of making intentional associations in order to improve learning retention. What do we mean by "intentional associations"?

   When learning, a person continually makes associations. We make associations between what we are learning and the environment we are in, between the information and our mental states, and between the information and our stream of thoughts.

When things are associated in memory, thinking of one helps bring another to mind. Have you ever actually retraced your path when you have forgotten where you put an object such as your keys?

Often, as you approach the place where you put them, you are suddenly able to remember the act of laying them down on the table or putting them in your purse. This is association. The memory of putting the keys down was associated with your memory of things in the environment.

You can make associations work for you by making them intentional. When you are having difficulty recalling new material, you can help bring it to mind by thinking about what you have associated it with. In other words—retrace your mental path. We will return to this idea later when we discuss specific strategies.

Deep processing – Relating the material to yourself. One way to process information more deeply, and also to create meaningful associations, is to think about how the information can be personally meaningful. You might think about how the new material relates to your life, your experience or your goals. If you can link new information to memories already stored ("mental hooks"), you'll have more cues to recall the new material.

Grouping – This idea is probably best explained with an example. Before reading ahead, take a moment to complete the following exercise.

Exercise: Grouping

Read the following list of sports one time. When you are done, write down as many of the sports as you can without looking back at the list.

Snow Skiing

Basketball

Tennis

Long Jump

100-Metre Dash

Hockey

Baseball

Ice Skate

Discus

Golf

High Jump

Volleyball

Javelin

Soccer

Swimming

Cricket

Decathlon

Hurdles

Polo

Note the number of sports you remembered correctly. We will return to this exercise later.

You can organize material by grouping similar concepts, or related ideas, together. Arranging the material into related groups helps your memory by organizing the information.

For example, in the exercise you just completed, you could have grouped all of the sports into one of the following categories:

a. Winter sports.

b. Track and Field sports.

c. Sports using a ball.

Keeping these categories in mind, try the exercise again. You will be able to remember more of the sports. You could try to create more categories to break the list into smaller pieces. That will help you memorise it better.

Of course, in this instance, we created a list with the intention of demonstrating grouping; thus, there were 6 or 7 sports in each category. Still, with a little thought, this strategy can be used in a variety of ways. For example, can you think of other ways that these sports could be grouped?

There are individual sports, team sports, sports you may enjoy, and sports you may dislike. There are sports requiring a great deal of equipment, and sports requiring little or none. When you are trying to remember lists for a test, the concepts and words may or may not have a natural organization. Therefore, you may need to be creative when making associations. Finally, the process of organizing a list into groups can often help you to understand the relationship between the concepts better.

4. **Vivid Associations** – We have already discussed the idea of associations: aiding storage and retrieval of new information by intentionally pairing it with something familiar.

When learning something new and unfamiliar, try pairing it with something you know very well, such as images, puns, music, whatever. The association does not have to make logical sense.

Often it is associations that are particularly vivid, humorous, or silly that stay in your mind. Some people remember names this way. For example, they may remember the name "Bharat Dube" by picturing Bharat drowning in the sea (*Dube* in Hindi means drowned), flailing his arms about, as it creates a humorous effect which will help them remember his name.

Or suppose for your anatomy course you have to recall names of the veins in the human body, and the first one on the list is "pancreatic" followed by "right gastroepipeloic" and "left gastroepipeloic" and so on. You can picture a frying pan being creative—maybe painting a picture with bright paints and bold strokes. If the frying pan is working in a studio, picture gas pipes with little padlocks on them (gastroepipeloic) in the left and right studio corners....

Exercise

Vivid Associations: Learning the Names of Classmates

Pick names of classmates with whom you are unfamiliar.

For each name, brainstorm some words or ideas that you can associate with the name. For example, if one student's name is Teresa Martin, you might think of Mother Teresa, a Martin (a type of bird), Mars the planet, a Martini (the drink), etc.

Once you have brainstormed several ideas, you can begin to think of ways that some of the associations can be combined to remember the name. In the above example, you could create a visual association by picturing Mother Teresa drinking a Martini.

Do this for each person, and you will have a great way to remember the names of your new classmates!

5. **Active Learning** – You will notice that the term "active learning" has come up frequently. Active learning facilitates your memory by helping you attend to and process information. All of the memory techniques we have discussed, require active learning. Even if you read a document carefully, there is no guarantee that you will learn and remember the information. Although you may passively absorb some material, to ensure that you remember important information requires being active and involved. And that means attending to and thinking about what you are learning.

6. **Visual Memory** – There are many ways of visually encoding and retrieving information. We have already mentioned the strategy of associating concepts with visual images. But other aids to visual memory include diagrams, tables, outlines, etc. Often these are provided in texts, so take advantage of pictures, cartoons, charts, graphs, or any other visual material. You can also draw many of these things yourself. For example, try to visualize how the ideas relate to each other and draw a graph, chart, picture, or some other representation of the material. You may even want to make it a habit to convert difficult material into actual pictures or diagrams in your notes, or to convert words into mental images on the blackboard of your mind.

   Finally, using your visual memory can be as simple as writing out vocabulary words, theories, or algebraic formulas. This allows you to not only practise (repeat) the information but also to see the way it looks on the page (developing a visual memory that you may be able to retrieve later). Another advantage is that it helps you take an active role in learning the material. When you draw your ideas on paper or write down things you are trying to remember, you have the opportunity to think about the information more deeply.

7. **Talk it Out** – When trying to memorize something, it can help to actually recite the information aloud. You might repeat ideas verbatim (when you need to do rote memorization), or you can repeat ideas in your own words (and thus ensure that you have a true understanding of the information).

Repeating information aloud can help you encode the information (auditory encoding) and identify how well you have learned it. Some students have told us that they know the test information and are surprised when they "freeze" and cannot give adequate responses. For some students, this "freezing" may be a result of test anxiety. For others, however, it may be a result of overestimating how well they know the material. If you recite the information aloud from memory (answering questions, defining words, or using flash cards), it is often quite clear how well you know it. If you stumble in your responses, or you have to look up for answers, or you can only give a vague kind of response, then you know that you need to study more.

Although reciting aloud can be a helpful memory technique, some people avoid it out of fear of appearing foolish ("what if someone sees me talking to myself?"). If this applies to you, work with a friend or study group. Another advantage of working with someone else is that they can inform you when you are missing important concepts or misunderstanding an idea. Keep in mind, however, that studying with others does not work for everyone. For example, some students may become anxious or intimidated in study groups and would be more comfortable studying alone.

8. **Visualize Yourself Teaching the Material** – An effective way to enhance recall and understanding of dense material is to teach it to an imaginary audience. By doing so, you are forced to organize the material in a way that makes sense to you and to anticipate potential questions that may be asked by your students. Moreover, by articulating your lecture aloud, you will uncover gaps in your comprehension (and recall) of the material. (Far better to discover those "weak" areas before a test than during it.) After you have mastered a particular section from your textbook, try delivering an organized lecture on any topic from that section. Then check for accuracy. Don't forget to anticipate questions that students might ask about the material as a way of anticipating potential test questions.

Using Strategies Effectively

You can predict how well a student will do from their use of study strategies. Forget intelligence. Forget hours put in. What's important is the effective use of good study strategies. To use a strategy effectively, you need to understand why it works, how it works, when it works and when it doesn't. For example, all students take notes — not everyone knows how to do it well. Research into the effectiveness of note taking has found — surprise, surprise — that sometimes note-taking helps you remember information, and sometimes it doesn't.

Effective note taking is more complex than simply knowing some strategies. Every learning situation is different. Every piece of text is different. Every lecture is different. It's not enough to have a stock way of organizing your notes, and to try and push all the information that comes your way into that format. Sometimes a matrix structure might be the best, sometimes a multimedia summary, sometimes a map, sometimes standard old linear notes. It depends on the information and it depends on how it is packaged.

The only way to know which strategy to use when is to understand how they work.

For example, the primary value of note taking is to select out the important information and connect it to other pieces of information. If you think the function of note taking is simply to record what someone has said, or what you've read, then your note taking will be far less effective.

Rules for Effective Note-Taking

Select. Omit trivial and redundant details. Omit anything you'll recall anyway!

Condense. Replace lists with a category term.

Organize. Choose headings and topic sentences.

Rephrase. Use your own words.

Elaborate. Make connections to existing knowledge.

To use note taking effectively, you need to understand that its primary value is not in the record you produce; it is in the process itself. The process of taking notes guides the memory codes you make. Note taking is a strategy for making information meaningful. It is therefore only effective to the extent that you paraphrase, organize and make sense of the information while taking notes.

Note taking is a strategy for making information meaningful. What does that mean?

What does it mean to make information meaningful? It means to connect new information to existing knowledge. The more connections you make, the better you will understand the information.

Connection is the heart of what makes information meaningful.

Why is it important to make information meaningful? Because, connection is the key to remembering. The more connections you have, the more entry points you have to the information, the easier it will be to retrieve. The facts, that you already know very well and have no trouble remembering them, act as anchor points.

The more anchor points you can connect to, the more meaningful the new information becomes, and the more easily you will remember it. Think about it for a moment. When you are told something new, you only understand it to the extent that you can relate it to something you already know.

It's like learning a new word. Pediment, for example. If you were told this was a triangular part crowning the front of a building in the Grecian style — assuming you don't already know the word, and assuming you have no particular knowledge of architecture — you're not likely to remember it without repeatedly coming across it. You might make the connection, pediment — impediment, but since there is no meaningful connection between these words, this won't help you remember the meaning of pediment. It might help you remember, the word itself. But to remember the meaning of the word, you need a meaningful connection. That might be provided by the suggestion that pediment is derived from a corruption of pyramid, which as we all know, is triangular, and is also a building. The more connections to existing anchor points, the more meaningful the word becomes, the more easily remembered it is. Connection is the key to remembering. The more connections you have, the more entry points you have to the information. Therefore, the more easily it will be found.

While note taking, ask yourself: does this help me make connections? Does it help me connect the facts together? Does it help me connect the new information with information I already have? Does it make any connection with facts I already know very well, and am unlikely to forget?

Conditions for effective note-taking
- Slow or self-determined rate of presentation
- Well-organized material
- Material that is not too difficult or complicated

What makes good notes?

To know this, we need to know what note-taking is really about. Most people think it's about recording information, and certainly that is part of its function — but the main value of note taking as a strategy for remembering information lies elsewhere:

Note-taking is a strategy for making information meaningful.

Here is an example. These are some notes on the water cycle:

Hydrological (water) Cycle

Precipitation & flow: "Whether they are typhoons or Scotch mists, mountain torrents or field ditches or city sewers, they are simply water sinking back to base level, the sea."

Evaporation = the act of passively presenting water to the atmosphere to be soaked up + vaporized by the sun's energy.

Transpiration = evaporation through plants. Plant draws water from ground through roots up to open-pored vessels in leaves, from where it is vaporized.

Condensation: as warm air rises it cools $-7°C$ every 1000m until it can't hold its cargo of water vapour any longer. It condenses into clouds, which cool further, condensing further into raindrops.

Warm front: when warm air advances on cold it rises over it.

Cold front: when cold air advances on warm + forces it to rise.

In this example, the notes are neat and tidy, with headings and indentations showing a degree of organization. Terms are defined. The notes appear to encapsulate the main ideas. A few abbreviations are used. These points are all widely cited recommendations for effective note-taking.

Memory and Related Learning Principles
The Principles of Short-Term and Long-Term Memory

This principle of long-term memory may well be at work when you recite or write the ideas and facts that you read. As you recite or write you are holding each idea in mind for the four or five seconds that are needed for the temporary memory to be converted into a permanent one. In other words, the few minutes that it takes for you to review and think about what you are trying to learn is the minimum length of time that neuroscientists believe is necessary to allow thought to go into a lasting, more easily retrievable memory.

Recognition is an easier stage of memory than the recall. For example, in an examination, it is much easier to recognize an answer to a question if five options are listed, than to recall the answer without the listed options. But getting beyond just recognizing the correct answer when you see it, is usually necessary for long-term memory, for the more we can recall about information the better we usually remember it.

Understanding new material. First and most important, you must make sure that you understand new material before trying to remember it. A good technique to ensure understanding is to recite or write the author's ideas in your own words. If you cannot, then you do not understand them.

The conclusion: you cannot remember what you do not understand. In other words, you cannot form a clear and correct memory trace from a fuzzy, poorly understood concept.

In the classroom, do not hesitate to ask the instructor to explain further any point that is not clear to you. If the point is unclear to you, there is a good chance that it is unclear to others, so you will not be wasting anyone's time. Furthermore, most instructors appreciate the opportunity to answer questions.

Getting it right the first time. We have learned that all remembering depends on forming an original, clear neural trace in the brain in the first place. These initial impressions are vitally important because the mind clings just as tenaciously to incorrect impressions as it does to correct impressions. Then we have to unlearn and relearn. Incorrect information is so widespread that Mark Twain once wrote, "Education consists mainly in what we have unlearned."

Evaluate the Learning. Another way to improve retention is through evaluation. After you have studied, work the matter over in your mind.

Examine and analyse it; become familiar with it like a friend. Use comparison or contrast: how is this topic like or different from related topics? If the learning concerns imaginary things, do you tend to agree or disagree? Are there aspects of the subject, which you can criticize? Analytical thinking encourages you to consider the matter from various aspects and this kind of mental manipulation makes you more knowledgeable. For all these reasons, recall is significantly improved.

The Principle of Over-Learning

After you have recited a lesson long enough to say it perfectly, if you continue reciting it a few times more, you will over-learn it. A well-known psychologist and researcher, Ebbinghaus, has reported that each additional recitation (after you really know the material) engraves the mental trace deeper and deeper, thus establishing a base for long-term retention. For many people over-learning is difficult to practise because, by the time they achieve bare mastery, there is little time left and they are eager to drop the subject and go on to something else. But reciting the material even just one more time significantly increases retention, so try to remember this and utilize the technique when you can.

The Principle of Recitation

There is no principle that is more important or more effective than recitation for transferring material from the short-term memory to the long-term memory. For one thing, you are obviously in the process of repeating the information. Recitation can take several forms—thinking about it, writing it out, or saying it out loud. "Thinking about it" is potentially the least effective because it gives us the least amount of reinforcement since writing or speaking involve more electrical-muscle movement messages to the brain which are known to increase mental response and recording. Vocal, "out loud" recitation is usually the most effective single technique for review because it employs more of the senses than any other review technique (utilizing both auditory and vocal senses.) If, for example, you review your notes immediately after class by vocal recitation, you will not only be consolidating the new information but also strengthening the neural traces made to your brain.

What is recitation? Recitation is simply saying aloud the ideas that you want to remember. For example, after you have gathered your information in note form and have categorized and clustered your items, you recite them.

Here's how: you cover your notes, and then recite aloud the covered material. After reciting, expose the notes and check for accuracy. You should not attempt to recite the material word for word; rather your reciting should be in the words and manner that you would ordinarily use if you were explaining the material to a friend. When you can say it, then you know it. (This is why it is best NOT to recite directly from the text.)

How Recitation Works

Recitation transfers material to the secondary or long-term memory. While you are reading the words in a sentence or paragraph, the primary memory (short-term memory) holds them in mind long enough for you to gain the sense of the sentence or paragraph. However, the primary memory has a very limited capacity, and as you continue to read, you displace the words and ideas of the initial paragraphs with the words of subsequent paragraphs. This is one reason for not remembering everything in the first part of the chapter by the time we reach the end of the chapter when we read continually without taking a break or taking time to review what we have already read.

It is only when we recite or contemplate the idea conveyed by a sentence or paragraph that the idea has a chance (not guaranteed) of moving on into the secondary memory (a long-term storage facility).

All verbal information goes first into the primary memory (short-term memory). When it is rehearsed (recited), part of it goes into our secondary (long-term) memory. The rest of it, usually the part we are least interested in, returns to the primary memory and is then forgotten. Whether new information is "stored" or "dumped" depends, then, on our reciting it out loud and on our interest in the information.

Remembering

According to several recent studies, learning which involves memorization of a unit of material begins slowly, then goes faster, and finally levels off. In other words, the amount learned per unit of time is small at first, then increases, and then becomes small again. These finding contrasts with older studies, which showed that learning was rapid at first, then became slower until it levelled off.

Even though a person continues to study, he may expect to encounter periods when there seems to be little or no gain. Such plateaus in learning may be due to several causes such as fatigue, loss of interest, or diminishing returns from using the same inefficient methods. Another explanation of plateaus is that they represent pauses between stages of understanding; when the student acquires a new insight, he can move on. Sometimes the lower stage of an understanding or a skill may actually interfere with progress to a higher level. For example, learning to read by individual letters of the alphabet interferes with learning to read by words. Learning to read word-by-word delays reading by phrases or sentences.

The important thing is to recognize that plateaus or periods of slow learning are inevitable, and they should not discourage the student unduly. Learning may still be taking place, but at a slower pace. Recognizing that he is at a plateau, the student should first try to analyse and improve his study methods, if possible. Sometimes, however, an incorrect mental set may be interfering with the necessary perception of new relationships. Sometimes slow learning may simply be due to fatigue. In either of these circumstances the most efficient procedure may be to drop the activity temporarily and return to it later, after a good night's rest.

The rate at which a student learns depends upon his learning ability, but slow learners remember just as well as fast learners, provided that they have learned the material equally well. The reason a bright student may do better on examinations is that he has learned the subject matter more effectively within the time available. But if a slower student spends enough time on his studies, he can retain every bit as much as the faster student. Fortunately, there is evidence that both rate of learning and rate of retention can be improved with practice.

The Principle of Neuro-Transmitter Depletion

Often students study or attempt to read for too long a period of time without stopping for a rest break. B.F. Skinner and other experts have concluded that the average student cannot usually study really difficult material efficiently for more than about four hours a day. Then efficiency and memory begin to suffer.

Research shows that the average student cannot study effectively on the same subject for more than about four consecutive hours, even with short breaks every hour. What occurs is what is referred to as The Principle of Neuro-Transmitter Depletion. Neuroscientists have developed techniques to monitor activity (usually defined as electrical impulses) and chemical changes in the brain during study or thought processing. If one studies the same subject too long, fatigue, boredom, sometimes a slight disorientation may occur. It is a common result of too much continuous study when even the simplest concept begins not to make sense any longer.

The monitoring of brain activity and chemical changes indicates that studying too long results in a depletion of chemicals in the brain cells necessary for efficient processing of information. Therefore, for effective consolidation of material into memory storage, take frequent breaks (at least 10 minutes every hour) and do not attempt to deal with really difficult material for more than about four hours a day, and do not study any easier subject area (even with breaks) for more than four consecutive hours.

Effective Learning

Just studying for long hours is not of any use unless it is accompanied by adequate learning. There are certain principles and guidelines, which can be used for effective learning. These are:

Persistence

Students often give up in despair when the answer to a problem is not immediately apparent. They crumple their papers and throw them away: "I can't do this," they say, "it's too hard." Or they write down any answer, just to finish the task as quickly as possible. They lack the ability to analyse a problem, to develop a strategy for attacking it.

When students gain persistence, they begin to use alternative strategies for problem solving. If they find that one strategy doesn't work, they know how to back up and try another, starting over if necessary. Over time, they develop systematic methods for analysing problems. They know how to begin, what steps must be performed, what data needs to be generated or collected – and how to keep going, without losing heart, until they have learned more about the problem.

Decreasing Impulsivity

Often, students blurt out the first answer that comes to mind. Sometimes they shout it out or start to work without fully understanding the directions. They may take the first suggestion given to them, or operate on the first idea that pops into their head. But as they gain intelligence they learn to consider alternatives and consequences of several possible decisions. They begin to reflect on their answers before talking; making sure they understand directions; planning a strategy for solving a problem; and listening to alternative points of view.

Listening to Others (With Understanding and Empathy)

Some psychologists believe that the ability to listen to another person, to empathise with and to understand another's point of view, is one of the highest forms of intelligent behaviour. Indications of listening behaviours include: being able to paraphrase another person's ideas, to empathise, and to accurately express another person's concepts, emotions and problems.

Children, without this form of intelligence, will ridicule, laugh at, or put down other's ideas.

Flexibility in Thinking

Some students have difficulty considering alternative points of view. Their way to solve a problem seems to be the only way. Their answer is the only correct answer. Instead of being challenged by the process of finding the answer, they are more interested in knowing whether their answer is correct. Unable to sustain a process of problem solving over time, they avoid ambiguous situations. A need for certainty outweighs an inclination to doubt. Their minds are made up, and they resist being influenced by any data or reasoning that might contradict their belief.

As students become more flexible in their thinking, they can be heard considering, expressing other people's points of view or rationales. While they progressively develop a set of moral principles to govern their own behaviour, they can also change their minds in the light of convincing data, arguments, or rationales. This ability makes it easier for them to resolve conflicts through compromise, to express openness about others' ideas, and to strive for consensus.

Metacognition (Awareness of Our Own Thinking)

Some people are unaware of their own thinking processes. When asked how they solved a certain problem, they cannot describe the mental steps that led them up to the act of problem solving. They cannot transform into words the visual images held in their minds. It is hard for them to plan for, reflect on, and evaluate the quality of their own thinking skills and strategies.

When students become more aware of their own thinking, they can describe what goes on in their heads, what they already know versus what they need to know, what data are lacking and their plans for producing those data. Before they begin to solve a problem, they can describe their plan of action, list the steps, and tell where they are in the sequence.

Here are Some Other Properties of Memory

Law of Recency

We are more likely to remember things that happened recently than those that happened a long time ago. You can probably remember what you had for dinner yesterday, but not what you ate for dinner two weeks ago.

Law of Vividness

We tend to remember the most spectacular or striking impressions rather than those that are more ordinary. You can probably remember what you did on your last birthday, or perhaps the Space Shuttle Challenger explosion, but not what happened on the previous day of those occasions (unless, that too, was a "special" occasion).

Law of Frequency

We tend to remember things we experience the most often, rather than those we experience only once in a while. You are much more likely to remember your name or your phone number than the square root of 3 (unless you are a mathematician).

∞

8. The Indian Approach on Memory

The Powerful Mind

The sages and yogis of our country were known to possess great control over the mind and were able to perform amazing feats through mind control.

How did They Do It?

The path to mind control is through deep concentration and meditation. If we want to harness the energies of our mind, we have to practise meditation. The world has awakened to this fact and more and more people, the world over, are taking to meditation to keep the body as well as mind in a healthy state.

It has already been proved that it is essential to be able to channelise the thoughts and focus the attention on the subject one wants to memorise. This can only be done through unwavering concentration.

How does One Create Deep Concentration?

Concentration is nothing but total attention to a subject. Our traditional philosophy towards learning is through total concentration developed by meditation. So, if one can learn meditation, one should be able to acquire the required power of concentration, which will make learning a very easy process. The main purpose is to keep distractions at bay.

I have a great admiration for Swami Vivekananda because of his mental process. He was one of the greatest men that India has ever produced. This country would have been a different one if there were just five Vivekanandas in it. Not only was he brilliant as far as mind power is concerned; he was a man of very strong convictions and faith. According to Swami Vivekananda, the human mind is an extraordinarily powerful entity.

Swami Vivekananda's Thoughts

Swami Vivekananda's thoughts on the mind power reinforce the Indian Philosophy on the subject. He says that the extraordinary powers are in the mind of man and this mind is a part of the universal mind. Human mind is capable of feats that are awe-inspiring. For example, Uri Geller is able to bend a metallic spoon or a rod just by staring it while his mind-power is focussed on the act. There are people who can control the movement of the blades of a fan by mind-power. These people are able to use more than the 10 percent brain-power generally used by most human beings.

I quote Swami Vivekananda from "The Complete Works of Swami Vivekananda" where he talks about the honing of the human mind through breathing and concentration.

"Have you ever noticed the phenomenon that is called thought-transference? A man here is thinking something, and that thought is manifested in somebody else, in some other place. With preparations – not by chance – a man wants to send a thought to another mind at a distance, and this other mind knows that a thought is coming and he receives it exactly as it is sent out. Distance makes no difference. The thought reaches the other man and he understands it. This shows that there is a continuity of mind, as the Yogis call it". "The mind is universal", said Vivekananda.

"The main difference between men and the animals is the difference in their power of concentration. All success in any line of work is the result of this. Everybody knows something about concentration. We see its results every day. High achievements in art, music, etc., are the result of concentration. An animal has very little power of concentration. Those who have trained animals find much difficulty in the fact that the animal is constantly forgetting what is told to him. He cannot concentrate his mind long upon anything at a time. Herein is the difference between man and animals – man has the greater power of concentration. The difference in their power of concentration also constitutes the difference between man and man. Compare the lowest with the highest man. The difference is in the degree of concentration. This is the only difference.

The great trouble with such concentration is that we do not control the mind; it controls us. Something outside of ourselves, as it were, draws the mind into it and holds it as long as it chooses.

If I speak to you well upon a subject you like, your mind becomes concentrated upon what I am saying. I draw your mind away from yourself and hold it upon the subject in spite of yourself. Thus our attention is held, our minds are concentrated upon various things, in spite of ourselves. We cannot help it.

Now the question is: Can this concentration be developed, and can we become masters of it? The Yogis say, yes. The Yogis say that we can get perfect control of mind. On the ethical side there is danger in the development of the power of concentration – the danger of concentrating the mind upon an object and then being unable to detach from it at will. This state causes great suffering. Almost all our suffering is caused by our not having the power of detachment. So along with the development of concentration we must develop the power of detachment.

This is the systematic development of the mind. To me the very essence of education is concentration of mind, not the collecting of facts. If I had to do my education over again, and had any voice in the matter, I would not study facts at all. I would develop the power of concentration and detachment, and then with a perfect instrument I could collect facts at will.

We should put our minds on things; they should not draw our minds to them. We are usually forced to concentrate. Our minds are forced to become fixed upon different things by an attraction in them, which we cannot resist. To control the mind, to place it just where we want it, requires special training.

In training the mind the first step is to begin with the breathing. Regular breathing puts the body in a harmonious condition; and it is then easier to reach the mind. In practising breathing, the first thing to consider is 'Asana' or posture. Any posture in which a person can sit easily is his proper position. The spine should be kept free, and the ribs should support the weight of the body. Do not try by contrivances to control the mind; simple breathing is all that is necessary in that line. All austerities to gain concentration of the mind are a mistake. Do not practise them.

The mind acts on the body, and the body in its turn acts upon the mind. They act and react upon each other. Every mental state creates a corresponding effect on the mind. It makes no difference whether you think the body and mind are two different entities, or whether you think they are both but one body – the physical body being the gross part and the mind the fine part. In the training of the mind, it is easier to reach it through the body. The body is easier to grapple with than the mind.

The finer the instrument, the greater the power. The mind is much finer and more powerful than the body. For this reason it is easier to begin with the body.

The science of breathing is the working through the body to reach the mind. In this way we get control of the body, and then we begin to feel the finer working of the body, the finer and more interior, and so on till we reach the mind. As we feel the finer workings of the body, they come under our control. After a while you will be able to feel the operation of the mind on the body. You will also feel the working of one half of the mind upon the other half, and also feel the mind recruiting the nerve centres; for the mind controls and governs the nervous system. You will feel the mind operating along the different nerve currents.

Thus the mind is brought under control – by regular systematic breathing, by governing the gross body first and then the fine body."

Basic Meditation

- Start by sitting comfortably in a quiet place with a minimum amount of disturbance.
- Close your eyes without straining them.
- Take a deep breath and settle down to normal breathing pattern. Breathe normally, naturally and gently; allow your awareness to be on your breathing process. Simply observe your breath, trying not to control it or alter it in any conscious manner.
- As you observe your breath, you may notice that it changes on its own accord. It may vary in speed, rhythm, depth and

116

sometimes it may even appear to stop for a time. Whatever happens with your breathing, innocently observe it without trying to cause or initiate any changes.

- You will find that your attention drifts away from your breath and you are thinking about other things or listening to noises outside. The mind constantly wanders, refusing to concentrate. Whenever you notice that you are not observing your breath, gently bring your attention back to your breathing.

- If during meditation, you notice that you are focusing on some feeling, mood or expectation, treat it as you would treat any thought and bring your attention back to your breathing.

- Practise this technique for about fifteen minutes.

- At the end of those fifteen minutes, keep your eyes closed and just sit quietly for 2-3 minutes. Allow yourself to come out of the meditation gradually before opening your eyes and resuming your normal activities for the day.

- Although no set time has been delineated for meditation, it is best done in the early morning, as there is a minimum distraction at that hour.

- Initially it will be difficult to hold the concentration for more than a few seconds and you will find your mind wandering constantly. But don't let that phenomenon instil a sense of defeat. Don't give up. If you continue the effort you will find yourself being able to increase the span of meditation. It is a slow but sure process.

You may find yourself experiencing some strange sensations, which are difficult to pen down. These are normal sensations and they denote that you are able to focus your energies.

- You may feel a sense of boredom or restlessness or your mind may become filled with thoughts of all kinds. Some of these thoughts may even be quite shameful ones. Don't get taken aback by them. This is an indication that the deep-rooted stresses and emotions are being released from your system. By effortlessly continuing with meditation, you will facilitate the removal of these impurities from your mind and body.

- You may even fall asleep. If you fall asleep in meditation, it is an indication that you need more rest during other times of the day. It also means that you have been neglecting the rest phase of your body and not heeding to its signals.
- You may slip into the 'gap' when the mantra or breath becomes very settled and refined. You slip into the gap between thoughts, beyond sound, beyond breath. This is also quite a natural process and one need not feel worried about these experiences.
- If you stay rested, take care of yourself and take time to commit to meditation. You are bound to get in touch with your inner self. You will tap the cosmic mind, the voice that whispers to you non-verbally in the silent spaces between your thoughts. This is your inner intelligence, and it is the ultimate and supreme genus that mirrors the wisdom of the universe. Trust this inner wisdom and all your efforts will come true.
- Success in meditation will give you an uplifting sensation, which is pure joy and bliss. It will make your soul feel light and happy and many bodily ailments like aches and pains will gradually disappear.
- You will be able to see a remarkable change in yourself and in your style of work. The efficiency will increase and your patience will also increase. Your dealings and relationships with other human beings will undergo a vast change. There will be a feeling of generosity and an all-pervading sense of joy.
- After several months of practising meditation successfully, you will begin to notice a gradual change in your personality.

9. Memory Improving Foods and Herbs

Memory Improving Herbs

The demands on us as individuals are high and the pressure to perform at our best is ever present. Success in professional and social situations comes easier to those who are able to focus, concentrate and learn information quickly. To be able to express our personality and sparkle in conversation, we must fluently and speedily recall the information we have learned. Not just in a rote fashion, but with the ability to pluck gems of loosely connected information from our mind, and to bring it all together in inspired flashes of inventive, creative, and witty conversation.

Having developed our skills to the highest level that our natural potential can reach, it would be sad to lose it all simply through neglect of keeping our brain and nervous system healthy.

There are herbs that can enhance your powers of memory and concentration. Including herbs in our daily regime is one way in which we can offer our body the required help to keep it healthier.

Here is a list of herbs that contain the qualities that we are looking for:

Ginkgo Biloba

One herb that has gained a strong reputation for its influence on the brain, and especially on memory, is ginkgo biloba. It is a tree, which has existed for millions of years, and which has been used since ancient times for its ability to improve memory and concentration. Clinical studies have clearly shown that Ginkgo has the power to address cerebral insufficiency, which often affects an individual with absent mindedness, poor memory, lack of concentration, decreased physical performance, etc. Ginkgo has also been found very effective in treating age-related memory impairment.

Ginkgo increases the rate at which information is transmitted at the nerve-cell level. Ginkgo increases circulation, especially the circulation in tiny blood vessels, such as those in the brain. It dilates blood vessels by releasing a vessel-relaxing factor. This characteristic is able to improve oxygen and nutrient delivery to the brain, and is one of the reasons that ginkgo has gained a reputation for increasing memory.

The leaves of the Ginkgo biloba tree, also known as the maidenhair tree, have been used for more than 5,000 years for medicinal purposes. It's one of the most widely used herbal extracts in Europe, and has been approved by the German government to treat symptoms of ageing, including cognitive disorders.

Ginkgo has been shown to have the following effects:
- Improve overall cognitive function and sharpen mental focus.
- Prevent and treat symptoms of dementia.
- Slow the progression of Alzheimer's in its early stages, and progressive decrease in symptoms of Alzheimer's disease.
- Treat "cerebral insufficiency", a slow decline in mental function associated with ageing and characterized by such symptoms as impaired concentration and memory, confusion, and mood disorders.
- Ginkgo works primarily by increasing blood flow and, consequentially, the supply of oxygen and nutrients to the brain. As a potent antioxidant, ginkgo helps protect against cellular damage.

Siberian Ginseng

Siberian ginseng is another quality herb that is beneficial to both the brain and the central nervous system. It is known as an "adaptogen" and serves to balance the internal organs. It has consistently demonstrated an ability to increase the sense of well-being in a variety of psychological disturbances, including depression, insomnia, hypochondrias and various neuroses.

Ginseng not only has powerful antioxidant properties, it has also been found to increase circulation which is associated with improved oxygen delivery and increased energy, similar to the effects of ginkgo biloba.

St. John's Wort

This is a herb that is rapidly becoming popular for its effects on mood and anxiety. Recent research indicates that St. John's wort may be acting by increasing levels of the "feel good" neurotransmitter called serotonin, which actually is "brain food". St. John's wort has been effectively used to control depression.

Brahmi (Bacopa monniera)

Brahmi was traditionally used to treat mental illness, including epilepsy. It can help strengthen memory, elevate brain function, increase concentration and mental focus, enhance mood and reduce the effects of stress. In India, it has long been incorporated in hair oils for massage. It has been used to provide a cooling effect to the scalp and to relax the nerves.

Brahmi contains substances called bacosides, which are responsible for improving memory and memory-related functions by enhancing the efficiency of nerve impulse transmission. Bacosides work by repairing damage to worn-out neurons.

Bilberry

Bilberry, long known for its ability to improve eyesight, can help brain function as well. By increasing circulation and blood flow, bilberry works in much the same way as ginkgo. Additionally, it's a potent antioxidant and can prevent free radical damage to the brain.

Ginger

Has the ability to improve the circulation and to support the central nervous system. It acts as a catalyst herb for other herbs, which are more specific in addressing memory and concentration. It helps them to do their work more effectively.

Gotu Kola

This herb is suggested for improving thought clarity and memory. It is also considered excellent for promoting a feeling of calm and stress relief.

Gotu Kola is the most widely used herb in Indian (ayurvedic) Medicine. Traditionally used as a nerve tonic and a general tonic in times of physical and mental exertion, it is also widely used to assist in pain relief of arthritis. In ayurvedic medicine, the herb is also used for ailments of the nerves and mind including epilepsy, schizophrenia and memory loss. The Chinese value Gotu Kola more as a plant that increases longevity and brain capacity than for any other purpose.

It is able to rebuild energy reserves and for this reason it is called 'food for the brain'. It increases mental and physical power. It combats stress and improves reflexes. Gotu Kola has an energising effect on the cells of the brain and is also said to help prevent nervous breakdown. It can relieve high blood pressure, mental fatigue and senility and helps the body defend itself against various toxins. It contains vitamins A, G, and K and is high in magnesium.

Some sources indicate that massive doses of Gotu Kola can produce narcotic effects. The evidence for this effect is sketchy at best and is controversial. No toxic effects are listed and Gotu Kola is considered to be quite safe by nearly all herbalists.

Ho Shou Wu – In traditional Chinese medicine, Ho Shou Wu is considered an excellent tonic herb, which supports and calms the nervous system. It is considered appropriate for increasing energy levels due to its nutritive actions.

Linden – Linden flowers are often recommended for their soothing actions and ability to transform restlessness into productive concentration.

Rosemary – It is an excellent antioxidant herb, which has traditionally been used to enhance and improve memory capabilities. It is considered a very good brain 'tonic', and is recommended for addressing headaches, especially those of a nervous tension origin.

Kelp – It is one of the very best sources available for minerals. Kelp supplies the body with many of the nutrients required by all body systems, including the brain. When adequate supplies of vitamins and minerals are available, the body can function at a better level, with mental clarity and better mental performance.

Betony – It is considered to be a very good nervine herb, which offers relief from anxiety and tension. Betony is a cerebral relaxant, that helps to calm a stressful mind.

Peppermint – It is a traditional herb that is always a topic of research studies. Peppermint is useful for tension-related headaches. It is also considered to be very helpful in promoting mental clarity.

Rehmannia – This is often used as a tonic in traditional Chinese medicine to relieve nervousness and calm the heart. It is also believed to act preventively against senility.

Skullcap – It is an excellent herb which offers relief from nervous irritability and tension. It is considered useful for reducing worry and anxiety, thus allowing for clearer and more precise thinking processes.

Flower Essences – Flower therapy is a method of treating various psychological and emotional imbalances to prevent their manifestation as physical illness. Flower therapies may be helpful in treating various types of mental disorder, including anxiety, depression and stress. One study on flower essences showed that the flower therapy was effective on nearly 90 percent of subjects. Flower essences are thought to work by encouraging a more balanced emotional and mental state.

Herbs should be an integral part of a healthy diet and lifestyle plan, which also includes adequate exercise and relaxation techniques. This information is intended for educational purposes only and is not intended to diagnose, treat or cure.

Sunflower Seeds Help your Memory

Do you always forget where you placed your keys or your purse? What about Mr. What's His Name, that very kind acquaintance who referred you to your next job? What was the name of the movie you saw last week? If you're blaming genetics or stress on your memory challenge, you might be pointing your finger in the wrong direction.

The major clue to your forgetfulness may be linked to what you store in your body, not in your short-term memory bank.

Clinical tests continue to show that people with adequate levels of the B Complex Vitamin Riboflavin do well on memory exams. The "B" could stand for "brain," if you're one of many with limited instant recall. And the best source of that vitamin is sunflower seeds.

Even when you're sleeping or relaxing, your brain is still hard at work. Although it makes up just two percent of your total body weight, it uses up to 30 percent of your daily intake of calories. For it to work properly, it must be fed. Even if you're not a breakfast eater, that meal is the best way to jumpstart your brain. A quick and easy sandwich with peanut butter, an orange, and a glass of milk might be what your brain may be asking you first thing in the morning when you feel like your head is in a fog. Snacking on sunflower seeds and fruit between meals adds more muscle to that hungry, demanding tissue.

Thiamine, or Vitamin B-1, also helps the memory; and that's found in cereals, meats and nuts. Zinc is still recognized as a crucial brain mineral, and scientists have discovered that even a mild deficiency of this nutrient can affect both memory and mental functions. Good sources of zinc include dark turkey meat, whole grains and seafood. Research also shows that the mineral Boron has an effect on the brain's electrical activity. Foods, high in Boron, include broccoli, apples, pears, peaches and grapes. In Chinese culture, walnuts are known as the longevity fruit because it is believed that they feed both the kidneys and the brain. And according to Chinese philosophy, if you keep those two vital organs in good working order, you'll live longer.

In essence, if you need help in remembering, just keep in mind the letter "B." Vitamin B-1, Vitamin B Complex and Boron all help you to "bear in mind" even on those days when life's challenges are driving you crazy or getting on your nerves.

Brain Food

In the recent years a lot of research has gone into finding food, which can keep the brain cells working at their optimum level. The market is flooded with packages designed to provide food to promote intelligence.

Eating for the Grey Cells

Food has a strong connection with your mental faculties. Surprised? Well, researches have proved that certain kind of foods play a very significant role in the improvement of memory and keeping the brain cells active.

For a long time it has been said that fish was a brain food. In fact, most of us grew up hearing that the Bengalis were an intelligent lot because they consumed fish everyday. Whether the Bengali brain has anything to do with fish eating habits or not is debatable, but there is some truth in the presumption that fish has an effective role to play in keeping the brain functioning at its optimum level.

The food that we eat everyday has a massive influence on the functioning of the brain and keeping it fit for performance. Elements like diet with low nutrients, exposure to the environmental toxins in our everyday living, stress, working round the clock against the dictates of our body clock, constant intake of stimulants like alcohol, tobacco, caffeine and junk foods to keep us going, all have an enormous effect on our mental functions.

Brain is the master control centre of the body. It is constantly active, receiving information from the senses about conditions both inside the body and outside it. It is burdened with the enormous task of rapidly analysing all the information and then sending out messages that control body functions and actions. The brain also stores information from past experience; which is possible for us to learn and remember. In addition, the brain is the source of thoughts, moods and emotions. The human brain consists of billions of interconnected cells that enable people to use language, solve difficult problems, and create works of art.

Brain Facts

The human brain weighs about 1.4 kilograms. It is about 2 percent of the total body weight but it uses about 20 percent of the oxygen that is used by the entire body while at rest. Most of the brain cells are present from birth and so the increase in weight comes mainly from growth of these cells. During the first six years of a person's life, he learns and acquires new behaviour patterns at the fastest rate in life. A network of blood vessels supplies the brain with the vast quantities of oxygen and food that it requires to keep functioning.

Although memory and the loss of it is a complex and mysterious process, there is constant research going on in the field to solve the unknown processes that lead to a good or a bad memory. Scientists know very little about what happens in the brain when it stores memories. But, they are almost certain that storing new memories involves both chemical changes in the nerve cells of the brain and changes in their physical structure. The researches in this field indicate that these chemical and physical changes occur in a tiny section of the brain, called the hippocampus, when a person stores new information. Scientists have discovered that memory is acquired by means of a series of solidifying events in the brain.

If it were as easy as changing the hard disk of a computer to accommodate more memory, life would have been so easy. All one had to do was to upgrade the memory chip and hey presto! We would have a completely efficient system of retaining memory, forever. Unfortunately, the brain is not a computer chip.

Brain Fatigue

The brain is the largest consumer of the energy that our body produces. To process information efficiently, to access important data, and to store necessary information, it needs oxygen, glucose and other nutrients. Lack of these leads to short-term memory loss and mental fatigue.

Memory loss occurs due to a whole lot of reasons. Although it primarily happens due to disuse, stress too can lead to forgetfulness. Clinical factors can also take their toll on the brain. Certain medications have side effects on the brain and cause fogginess and lack of concentration. Nutrition can affect the brain's working. The kind of food you eat can aggravate your mental inefficiencies. Thus it is very important to maintain a healthy food diet including all the nutrients necessary for the proper functioning of the brain.

The Food Factor

Just like every organ in the body, the brain needs to be fed. If it doesn't get a constant supply of glucose for energy, it lets us know. Symptoms of sluggishness, lethargy, dizziness and even fainting can occur if we don't feed the brain.

The free radicals generated by the body can lead to erosion in the functioning of the brain. The waste products released by the body when we burn food for energy production is the free radical phenomenon. These free radicals can often lead to some loss of memory over the years.

What are Free Radicals?

In a perfect world, everything works together in harmony to create lush, productive, and beautiful landscapes. Energy is balanced and synergy abounds. The same idea applies to health when our bodies are fit and in chemical balance. But today's world is far from perfect. Our lives are typically stressful and we consume toxins on a daily basis, which ultimately alter our delicate biochemistry and wreak havoc on our trillions of internal chemical reactions. Compromised immune systems and increased exposure to free radicals eventually wear us down, age us prematurely, or bring on fearful diseases like cancer. But powerful natural compounds called antioxidants form a front line of defence that attack and neutralize the hordes of free radicals, helping us restore our health and live longer, happier lives.

Free radicals and antioxidants are two words that we are increasingly hearing in context of health and ageing. Few of us really understand these terms. Let us try to get a clearer picture about antioxidants and free radicals.

A freshly cut apple will turn brown in a matter of minutes. Iron, when exposed to water and air, starts to rust. These chemical changes are the result of oxidation, the process by which a compound reacts with oxygen. Oxidation in the body creates free radicals in the fats, tissues, and bloodstream. The higher the number of free radicals, the greater the level of oxidative stress.

Oxygen is a critical element in the water we drink and the air that we breathe—without it we could not survive. Yet normal cellular reactions create toxic forms of oxygen that are free radicals such as super oxide, hydroxyl and lipid peroxides, singlet oxygen, and hydrogen peroxide. Small amounts of free radicals in the body are a good thing - too many, however, accelerate ageing and disease.

Not all free radicals are bad. Free radicals produced by the immune system destroy viruses and bacteria. Others are involved in producing vital hormones and activating enzymes that are needed

127

for life. But most of us are bombarded by a number of environmental toxins like smog, cigarette smoke, heavy metals, gasoline derivatives, ultraviolet radiation, and other carcinogenic chemicals that are also sources of free radicals. A healthy body can normally keep its free radicals in check, but if the immune system is weakened or the free radical load is too high, it results into cellular damage.

A significant cause of ageing is cellular free radical damage. As we get older, an increased amount of free radical garbage accumulates in our bodies. The good thing is that we are not completely powerless. Antioxidant supplements can help to protect us from the damage of free radical bombardment.

How Antioxidants Work?

Antioxidants are compounds that neutralize free radicals by giving them the necessary electron they crave for. Antioxidants can be vitamins, minerals, hormones, or enzymes. Although a certain amount is manufactured in the body as enzymes or hormones, most of our antioxidants come from fruits and vegetables.

Although many antioxidants can be obtained from food sources, it is difficult to get enough of them to hold back the free radicals constantly being generated in our polluted environment.

Certain antioxidants protect specific parts of the body against certain kinds of free radicals. For example, vitamin E protects the fats in cell membranes. In addition to fighting free radicals, antioxidants stimulate the immune system, reduce inflammation and fever, and help control pain. Once an antioxidant neutralizes a free radical, it is essentially "spent."

Maintaining a healthy immune system, reducing stress, and consuming antioxidants can minimize free radical damage. Conditions that can be avoided or improved using antioxidant therapy include cancer, coronary heart disease, autoimmune disorders, rheumatoid arthritis, cataracts, diabetes, menopause, fertility, and neurological disorders such as Alzheimer's disease and Parkinson's disease.

Some Anti-Oxidant Sources

Vitamin C

Vitamin C is probably the most well-known antioxidant. It helps minimize free radical damage to the neurological system. It also protects other antioxidants in the body, such as vitamin E. In addition to neutralizing free radicals, vitamin C detoxifies the body, reduces high blood pressure, lowers cholesterol, and fights cancer. It has the beneficial effect on glutathione levels and helps prevent free radical damage to the brain cells. In the presence of high levels of glutathione, the body's immune system functions efficiently and prevents damage to the brain cells.

Vitamin A and beta-carotene

Both vitamin A and beta-carotene are powerful free-radical scavengers that protect the skin, mucous membranes, circulatory system, and help in controlling cholesterol levels. In particular, beta-carotene is very effective in neutralizing the singlet oxygen-free radical.

More than 600 different types of carotene have been identified from fruits and vegetables. Preliminary research indicates that alpha-carotene is up to 100 times more powerful as an antioxidant than beta-carotene. Others include lutein, gamma-carotene, zeaxanthin, and lycopene, a known cancer fighter that occurs in high concentrations in tomato products.

Vitamin E

This antioxidant prevents the oxidation of lipids (fats) in cell membranes, which strengthens the outer cell layers against free radical attack. Vitamin E works best in the presence of selenium, another antioxidant, and helps protect vitamin A. Vitamin E stimulates the immune system, improves the circulatory system and oxygen absorption, fights cancer, and has a role in preventing cataracts.

Vitamin E also helps to protect the brain against oxidative stress. An intake of about 400 mg every day can be very helpful.

Lycopene

There is no denying the fact that antioxidants are a significant part of the important nutrients we need today to support our health. One of the more newly understood of these antioxidants is lycopene. This much-hailed phytonutrient is found in tomatoes. It is actually the substance that gives tomatoes their red colour and, like beta-carotene, is a member of the carotene family.

While fresh tomatoes are loaded with lycopene, cooking them makes it even easier for our body to use their lycopene. Apparently, as the tomatoes break down when they are cooked, the lycopene is more easily absorbed. Including a little fat will help, too, especially mono-saturated fat like olive oil.

It is not known exactly how much lycopene one should consume each day, but based on recent studies, you would probably need to eat ten servings of tomatoes per week.

When you exercise heavily, you need additional antioxidants, according to a leading researcher. Exercise stimulates your body's production of "free radicals" that attack cells, leading to long-term damage and a higher risk of cancer. To counteract the exercise hazard, experts suggest taking antioxidant supplements daily, notably vitamin E (400 IU) and vitamin C (1000 mg).

Coffee

Brewed coffee seems to create hundreds of new chemicals that appear to have antioxidant qualities. Each chemical is present in only tiny amounts, but taken together in a cup of coffee, they could add up to have about the same antioxidant effect as three oranges. Cheers to the strong brew!

Selenium

Selenium is in news. Every health magazine and newspaper has been raving about its values. It has been found to be beneficial in the fight against free radicals, which contribute to premature ageing, among other things. Selenium is found in the highest concentrations in seafoods, grains, muscle meats, and Brazil nuts. A multi-vitamin that contains between 70-100 mcg is recommended, but an additional supplement is not necessary. It has also recently shown that selenium can help prevent cancer.

Zinc

Just like it protects your car from rust, zinc has antioxidant properties that protect the body. Zinc is required to maintain effective levels of vitamins E and A. It is also a key ingredient in the very important antioxidant enzyme called superoxide dismutase (SOD).

Pycnogenol

Pycnogenol is an effective antioxidant. Common sources are the bark of the French maritime pine tree (Pycnogenol), grape seed, lemon tree bark, peanuts, and cranberries. Research indicates that this compound may be 20-50 times more potent than vitamins C and E. Besides, it keeps joints and skin supple, and promote a youthful appearance. It also strengthens capillaries, improves circulation, reduces joint pain, and protects nerve tissue.

Other Plant Sources

Several popular supplements like bilberry, ginkgo biloba, and garlic are very strong antioxidants. Bilberry helps eliminate free radicals from capillary walls and red blood cells; it is also known to improve arthritis. Its ability to improve vision was first observed during World War II when it was discovered that British pilots, who ate bilberry jam, had excellent twilight vision.

Ginkgo biloba is famous for improving memory, partly because it contains antioxidants that scavenge free radicals and boost the effectiveness of vitamin C. It also improves circulation, heart conditions, and neurological disorders such as Alzheimer's disease.

Garlic contains high amounts of antioxidants, vitamin A, vitamin C, carotene, and selenium and boosts the levels of antioxidant enzymes in the bloodstream. Consuming a couple of cloves of garlic may keep your friends away but they definitely help to protect the neurons from damage.

Green tea also contains a variety of antioxidants, including catechin, and is known to lower cholesterol levels and reduce blood clotting. Is it a wonder that the Japanese, who consume so much of green tea, are so brainy?

What Really is Brain Food?

Once the free radicals have been taken care of, the brain will automatically function better. The other food elements that can be called brain food are -

- Vitamin B12 is known as the 'brain food' because of its contribution in maintaining the brain in a top form. It can be found in milk, chicken, fish, eggs, curds and cheese milk.
- Vitamin B12 helps in improving concentration and memory. As we grow older the body is unable to absorb enough B12 from food. This leads to neurological disturbances like loss of balance, muscle weakness, poor vision, mood disturbance and if the deficiency goes on over a period of time, it can

precipitate pseudo-senility, a condition that hampers memory retention. In such situation taking a supplement of Vitamin B12 can reverse the condition. The good sources of this vitamin are milk and milk products, red meat, eggs, fish and most non-vegetarian foods. Vegetarians have to resort to Vitamin B12 supplements in order to protect the brain from ageing effects.

- Vitamin B6, that is found in banana, wheatgerm, pulses, brown rice and brewer's yeast, is good for improving mood and promotes clear thinking.
- Nuts, like almonds and walnuts, are good brain food. Sesame seeds, soybeans, whole wheat and wheat germ, pumpkin seeds, lecithin and choline activate the brain and improve its performance.
- Citrus fruits, fresh fruits and carrots should form an essential part of your diet because they keep the brain alert.
- Certain herbs, like ginkgo, ginseng, and amino acids, like L-carnitine, prevent the degenerative condition of the brain and other vital organs. These elements are also known to have healing powers for the brain. They help in many ways like improving decision-making abilities, increasing attention span and mnemonic capacity. It is for this reason that many of the memory improving drugs available in the market today contain ginseng or ginkgo.
- For improvement in concentration and retention one should increase the intake of choline, lecithin, egg yolk and soya bean.

Smart Ways to Feed your Brain

In a world of ever-increasing information and growing demands on mental function, brain strain is not an uncommon occurrence. Fatigue is one of the most often cited complaints that sends people to their doctors and, increasingly, to the health food stores. As often as not, fatigue and a decline in mental alertness are the result of inadequate nutrients and oxygen in the brain, and a consequent decrease in brain function. Additionally, free radical damage seems to be a common theme in diminished neurological function. If you're feeling groggy and foggy, supplements can help. For optimal mental functioning, the brain, like any other organ, has certain basic requirements. The neurons in the brains are like all other cells in the body; each requires delivery of nutrients and oxygen, as well as removal of waste. Obviously, adequate circulation is paramount to ensuring brain health.

As we age circulation can be compromised to varying degrees. Certain supplements can boost circulation to ensure the adequate delivery of nutrients and oxygen. Ageing presents another problem: healthy brain function is related to flexible cell membranes, which allow the smooth flow and exchange of information. As the brain ages, cell membranes become rigid, thereby hampering the flow of information. Environmental factors and the rigours of everyday life present a big problem in the form of free radical damage.

Because free radicals are particularly attracted to fat cells, the brain, with its relatively high fat content, is especially vulnerable to free radical damage. Antioxidants help to stop the progress of free radicals before they can attack healthy cells- a scenario, which will ultimately result in diminished neurological function. In theory, a well-balanced diet should supply adequate amounts of antioxidants.

In reality, because of excess stress on the body and brain, environmental pollution and a reliance on processed foods, most people don't get enough antioxidants. For the ultimate brain protection, supplemental forms of antioxidants are advisable. Adequate nutrition is a major consideration for mental function. The brain is a relatively small organ, but it is a hungry one: the brain typically eats up about a quarter of the energy produced by the body. As such, it's exquisitely sensitive to nutrient deficiencies.

At the minimum, it must receive adequate nutrients to allow the synthesis and release of neurotransmitters. Mom's stories about brain food do have a basis in fact: fish, for example, is packed with compounds that help promote optimal mental functioning. The problem is, the most concentrated sources of brain nutrients are found in foods that most people have reduced or eliminated from their daily diets, like red meats, organ meats and eggs. But as awareness of the brain's nutritional needs grows, so do the number of supplements on the market.

A plethora of products that promise alertness and increased mental health function are available. Most work by either increasing circulation to the brain, providing nutrients for energy, or protecting the brain against the ravages of ageing. Some work by providing an instant boost through short-term stimulants.

B Vitamins

There are also many herbals and natural substances, which can help us, feed the brain and optimise its function. For instance, the B vitamins are extremely important in providing energy to the brain. The B vitamins are crucial enzymes for the metabolism of the glucose that gets translated into energy.

One of the most common indications of deteriorating brain function is memory loss. When many older people become aware of memory lapses, they jump to the conclusion that they are experiencing the early signs of Alzheimer's disease, when in fact their declining memory may be rooted in a nutritional deficiency.

In the mid-1940s and 1950s, scientific research clearly showed that healthy brain functioning depends on sufficient amounts of B vitamins. Experts still emphasise the importance of B vitamins, particularly the following five (keep in mind that these vitamins are all water-soluble and should be taken together for maximum benefit):

B1 (thiamine) helps convert glucose into energy.

Thiamine supplementation also appears to elevate mood. In a study, 120 young women were given either placebo or 50 mg thiamine daily for two months. Before-and-after tests were conducted to assess their mood, memory and reaction times.

The women who took the thiamine supplements reported feeling significantly more clearheaded, composed and energetic than the ones who were on placebo.

B3 (niacin) enhances the ability of red blood cells to carry oxygen. It is also vital to the formation and maintenance of many tissues, including nerve tissue. A severe niacin deficiency produces pellagra, a disease characterized by the three Ds: dermatitis, diarrhoea and dementia.

B6 (pyridoxine) is needed for the production of amino acid-derived neurotransmitters such as norepinephrine, serotonin and dopamine. B6 deficiency can cause many ailments including slow learning and visual disturbances. Low levels of this vitamin may also provoke epileptic seizures in people prone to them.

B12 (cobalamin) plays an important role in the formation of the myelin sheath around nerve fibres. It also helps the body transport and store folic acid. Vitamin B12 deficiency can cause pernicious anaemia, nerve dysfunction (weakness, poor reflexes and strange sensations in the arms and legs) and impaired mental activity. It has also been linked to depression, especially in the elderly.

Folic acid is necessary for DNA synthesis; hence it plays an essential role in all cell divisions and in the development of the foetal nervous system. As many as 31 to 35 percent of all depressed patients have folic acid deficiencies.

The Bs are also important for the reactions which power synthesis of our brain neurotransmitters, chemical signals that the brain uses to carry out physiological functions. B vitamins are needed for the synthesis of the neurotransmitters dopamine, norepinephrine and serotonin. Dopamine and serotonin are especially related to feelings of contentedness, well-being and satiety (fullness). Low levels of serotonin are associated with depression, anxiety and cravings.

Is Fish Really Brain Food?

The value of fish was recognised long before scientific studies proved the point. For centuries it has been seen as "brain food" and from the 1650s people have been taking cod liver oil to fight bone disease and aches and pains. Medical research has begun to confirm some of old physicians' practices and the old wives' tales. More recent studies have suggested that fish oil reduces the chances of heart problems, helps prevent hyperactivity in children, and is useful in treating depression, lowers aggression under stress and eases pain from arthritis. The role, fish oils may play in fighting cancer, especially breast cancer, is also under investigation.

Oily fish like salmon, kippers and tuna are especially beneficial. The importance of the oils lies not only in the protein, vitamin A - good for vision, hair, eyes and nails - vitamin D - good for teeth and bones - and trace elements such as phosphorus and iodine, but also in the large supplies of polyunsaturated fatty acids known as omega-3. This seems to help protect against heart disease by lowering levels of plasma triglyceride, which is associated with high cholesterol.

What about its Effects on the Brain?

Eating fish won't make you smarter than you already are, but it can help you rise to full mental potential when your brainpower is lagging.

Dr. Judith Wurtman, a distinguished food research scientist at MIT, has found that the high protein in fish, namely the amino acid tyrosine, can give a wonderful boost to the brain neurotransmitters norepinephrine and dopamine, thus energising your mind and making you feel more alert. This fish makes available to the brain the tyrosine, which is then used to make the brain-stimulating chemicals. This happens only when the norepinephrine and dopamine are being rapidly used up and your brain can take an extra jolt.

Thus, fish does not lift mental capacities further if your brain already has adequate supplies of the alertness chemicals. But if you have a special task to complete and want to ensure full power of your mind, choose fish for lunch or dinner. Dr. Wurtman puts fish on her 'A' list as a mental-energy-boosting food.

Which Kind of Fish?

While adding more fish to your diet appears healthful, it's important to note that not all fish are alike. Light-meat fish, like flounder or whiting, have only about 0.5 grams of omega-3 fatty acid per 4-ounce serving, while dark-meat fish, such as salmon, sardines, mackerel or bluefish, have roughly 1.5 grams of the protective fatty acid in the same amount of fish.

So, if you're going to eat only one serving of fish a week, experts recommend a dark-meat fish.

How Much of Fish?

Although consumption of fish was said to aid in reducing the risk of sudden death, it did not seem to change drastically with the increase in consumption. In other words, although eating fish once a week seemed to work, eating it more often did not work better. It should be taken broiled or grilled—not deep fried or doused with fat, which could ruin some of the effects.

Fruits and Vegetables are also Brain Food

It is common knowledge that fruits and vegetables are good for our health. We have always assumed that eating fruits and vegetables is good for health because they were good sources of a wide variety of vitamins (vitamin C in citrus fruit, vitamin A in carrots, folic acid in greens). When the fibre craze came along, it became important to eat fruits and vegetables because they were good sources of fibre. 100 grams of apple, for example, contains 2.7 g of fibre, while 100 grams of turnip contains 2.0 g of fibre. Fruits and vegetables also contain antioxidants and it is the effects of these dietary sources of antioxidants on brain that have an anti-ageing effect.

The brain is a strange organ. Firstly, because it is not as dynamic as other organs in the body—the turnover of cells in the brain is almost zero, unlike the liver or the lung. This means that the brain is particularly sensitive to the damage because once the brain-cells are injured or killed they aren't replaced. Secondly, it contains low concentrations of antioxidants. Antioxidants are known to be protectors of cells from a variety of environmental and metabolic disorders. Without the protection of antioxidants, the brain tissue is vulnerable to damage.

The phytochemicals in spinach and strawberry extract, particularly those with antioxidant properties, could provide protection against the onset of these degenerative diseases. However, experiments to prove their efficacy are difficult to carry out. Foods, such as spinach and strawberry extract, may be more effective than just pure vitamin E, because foods and extracts contain a cocktail of phytochemicals rather than just one active ingredient. A mixed diet with plenty of fresh fruits and vegetables is still probably the best dietary advice anyone can follow.

Memory Food

There is something you can do to help you maintain your mental strength for a long long time:

Eat! That's right, food can be a powerful cognitive aid. But not just any kind of food. One particular food group you should focus on to maintain your mental health is fruits and vegetables, and lots of them. In a study of elderly people, the participants, who consumed the most fruits and vegetables and the least fat and cholesterol, performed best on cognitive capacity tests. This is probably because fruits and vegetables are an excellent source of antioxidants, which help protect against free-radical damage to many of the body's cells including brain cells.

Almost any fruit or vegetable will contain these free-radical fighters, but blueberries and blackberries, in particular, are packed with brain-protecting antioxidants. Other nutrient-rich sources of antioxidants include prunes, raisins, garlic, kale, raw spinach, tomatoes and dried apricots.

Finally, if you're trying to ward off mental decline, a moderate amount of alcohol may be helpful, as long as you are not predisposed to addiction. A study of elderly people revealed that low to moderate alcohol consumption, about one drink per day, appears to protect against failing memory. Almost 30 percent of your daily calories feed your brain, so it's no wonder that food has such a great impact on the strength of your mind. Feed it right, and soon, not only will you feel smarter, but also you'll feel younger, no matter which birthday you have just celebrated.

The Final Word

One thing that all of us need to remember is that memory is not just about techniques and methods but it has a lot to do with self-confidence. If you feel that you can do it, you will be able to do it. There is nothing special about improving memory - anyone can do it. What one needs to remember is that a consistent and sincere effort made towards any self-improvement finally pays off. Insincere and half-hearted attempts, which end within a few weeks, do not make much difference.

There are no short cuts or instant cures for anything in this world. It is only persistence that works. Anything is possible if you want to do it; memory improvement is just a small drop in the ocean of self-improvement. But it is that drop, which is very significant, because it can change your entire life in terms of money, status, knowledge, relationship improvement and a horde of other things. So, tighten your belts, and get to work. And don't give up if you don't see significant results within a few weeks. The results will become visible over a period of time. Just keep at it!   OO

The Complete Guide to MEMORY MASTERY

—Harry Lorayne

ORGANISING & DEVELOPING THE POWER OF YOUR MIND

The memory is always present; ready and anxious to help if only we would ask it to do so more often. —Roger Broille

The more intelligible a thing is, the more easily it is retained in the memory, and contrariwise, the less intelligible it is, the more easily we forget it.

—Benedict Spinoza

Thinking is the hardest work there is, which is the probable reason why so few engage in it. —Henry Ford

Don't thou love life! Then do not squander time, for that is the stuff life is made of.
—Benjamin Franklin

Here, in one volume, you will learn his unique proven techniques to:
* Increase your powers of memory and concentration.
* Strengthen good habits and discard bad ones.
* Improve your powers of observation.
* Deliver a speech without fear.
* Become more organised, time-efficient.

Big Size • Pages: 312
Price: Rs. 160/- • Postage: Rs. 15/-

How to Develop A Super Power Memory

—Harry Lorayne

Tips to develop amazing memory capabilities

This is one of the all-time classics from the all-time best-selling author of memory-related books. Make your brain work for you. Scientists say we use only 10% of its capacity. Get the edge. Tap into your most precious resource and unleash the natural powers within you. You will never again have to be told anything twice...

TV infomercial star Harry Lorayne reveals his positive methods of developing a photographic memory. If knowledge is powerful then memory is super powerful! You will increase your memory capacity by tenfold and learn to accurately recall anything, anytime, anywhere — such as:
* Prices • Phone Numbers • Names
* Codes • Details • Facts
* Orders • Book Passages • Jokes
* Directions • Instructions
* Conversations • Dance Steps
* Dates/Places • Game Strategies
* Battle Plans • School Work
* Lectures • Speeches

Big Size • Pages: 168
Price: Rs. 135/- • Postage: Rs. 15/-

Boost Your Brain-Power

—Dr G Francis Xavier, PhD

Powerful techniques to develop super brainpower for successful living

Do you have an irresistible desire to accomplish something great and outstanding in life? Do you have a passion to develop Extraordinary Memory, Increased IQ, Imagination, Creativity and Visualisation? Do you wish to lead a happy, stress-free life with vibrant health? To achieve all this, you need to enhance the power of your brain, which is the master organ in the body.

Boost your Brainpower shows you the way by offering a variety of time-tested and proven techniques based on the ancient wisdom of the East, combined with practical modern research findings of the West, which include:

❖ Proper food, nutrition and supplements
❖ Exercises, both physical and mental
❖ Yoga, pranayama and meditation
❖ Boosting brainpower via puzzles, riddles and magic squares.

This is an invaluable book for all those who wish to lead a happy, enriched and successful life.

Demy Size • Pages: 144
Price: Rs. 96/- • Postage: Rs. 15/-

251 Study Secrets
from the Diary of a Top Achiever
—B.K. Narayan & Preeti Narayan

251 Easy & Practical ways to achieve greater success in studies

251 Study Secrets from the Diary of a Top Achiever provides you 251 easy methods and tricks to achieve top success in studies—without stress and tension. This unique 'quick help' book for students deals with all the topics that are important for your study success. Here are some of those topics:

❑ Confidence
❑ Motivation
❑ Choosing Career
❑ Fixing Goal in Mind
❑ Increasing Brainpower
❑ Program to Succeed
❑ Concentration
❑ Managing Time
❑ Becoming Healthy
❑ Learning More in Class

This book is written in short, concise form so that you can read fast, learn quickly, and use instantly! If you need more help visit: *www.mindpowerguide.biz*

Big Size • Pages: 164
Price: Rs. 150/- • Postage: Rs. 15/-

Sure Success in Interviews

—Jayant Neogy

This book's contents are far richer and deeper than other books on the subject. No contemporary book in the Indian market covers topics such as SWOT analysis, portfolio preparation, wardrobe tips, body language and interview preparation techniques that use question-and-answer sessions with analysis of top answers.

An exhaustive data bank of frequently asked questions and model answers ensures you hold an advantage over other candidates. Finally, there's a bonus section containing tips on good résumé writing practices.

A truly comprehensive, one-source guide that will turn you into a professional performer at any interview.

This book enables you to:

• How to write a winning résumé • Practical hints to overcome nervousness & boost confidence • SWOT (Strengths, Weaknesses, Opportunities & Threats) analysis • Portfolio preparation • Tips on wardrobe & self-grooming • Interview preparation techniques through Q&A sessions • The art of successful follow-up.

Demy Size • Pages: 200
Price: Rs. 96/- • Postage: Rs. 15/-

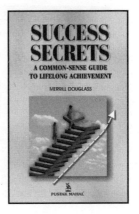

SUCCESS SECRETS
A Common Sense Guide to Life Long Achievement

—Merrill Douglass

Outstanding success is now within your reach — the keys to achieving it are in your hands! *Success Secrets* gives you *all* the powerful, life-changing guidance and direction you need to reach your full potential in your personal and professional life.

These dynamic success secrets won't just help you get to the top of your field, they'll enable you to get more of everything you want — on the job, in your relationships, and even in your leisure time. You'll master dozens of expert techniques for:

❖ managing your time ❖ setting reachable goals ❖ presenting a professional image ❖ getting ahead in your career ❖ leading effectively and much more!

A world-class course in achievement, this collection of super-motivating secrets will help you reach and exceed your loftiest dreams! You don't need a seminar on success. All you really need is *Success Secrets.*

Demy Size • Pages: 256
Price: Rs. 120/- • Postage: Rs. 15/-

The Portrait of a Super Student

—Abhishek Thakore

How best to perform in Studies, Sports & Co-curricular activities

Success today depends a lot on one's academic achievements. And to excel in studies, you don't have to be just an intelligent or brilliant student—but also one who knows how to manage studies and time. In fact even a mediocre or a below-average student can perform exceedingly well by following a scientific system.

The Portrait of a Super Student now brings you an innovative system specifically designed for super achievement. From simple, practical and time-tested tips on how to manage time, controlling temptation, scheduling time and work, relaxing techniques to diet control, speed reading, building vocabulary, improving presentation, discussing studies it goes on to guide how to make stress an ally, make a friend out of your TV and delaying gratification, besides others. And above all, to make it reader-friendly the book is divided into easy-to-read small chapters—with a practice section after every chapter.

Demy Size • Pages: 144 (colour)
Price: Rs. 110/- Postage: Rs. 15/-

Group Discussion For Admissions & Jobs

—Anand Ganguly

Does the aggressive speaker lead the way in a group discussion? Or the one who speaks more? Or the one who argues in favour of the subject?

Perhaps none! There are many myths prevalent about group discussions, and only the one who has seen it all from the other side of the table can guide you the right way! In this well-researched book, the author has put in the essence of his decades of corporate experience into a comprehensive and complete volume on the subject. Beginning from common myths about group discussions, the Do's and Don'ts of the test, he goes on to discuss at length about the prerequisites for preparation such as knowledge of the subject, importance of listening, presentation, initiation, body language, communication skills and co-operation.

In addition, the book offers you a comprehensive background on major relevant topics from generic drugs to pension reforms, from criminalisation of politics to sex education. Above all, you have 24 mock group discussions with detailed analysis and evaluation of speaker's approach and capability—offering an insight as to how to avoid the pitfalls and come out a winner.

Demy Size • Pages: 200
Price: Rs.108/- • Postage: Rs. 15/-

CAN is the word of POWER

—Barendra Kumar

"I liked you can yield a greater you....
My best wishes..."
—Dr. A.P.J. Abdul Kalam

Inspiration and motivation, undoubtedly increases effectiveness and efficiency. Thus, it is far more essential for the young minds of the nation than anybody else to help them DREAM BIG, AIM HIGH for improvements, innovations and inventions, which can be possible by strong positive thought, acquisition of creative/ inventive ideas and its execution according to strategic plan of action for the peace, progress and prosperity of self and society. CAN is... POWER not only advocates the same, but also covers all aspects of personal growth – spiritual, emotional, physical, mental, and inspires to make a successful career to build a meaningful life. Needless to say, it is equally useful for average to excelling students, as well as their custodians/well-wishers.

This book, for self-analysis, improvement and success, with hundreds of inspirational quotes and hints of stories of different event makers, from different countries — past and present — to expand the databank, will surely induce success thinking for better personal and national living.

Demy Size • Pages: 278
Price: Rs. 150/- • Postage: Rs. 15/-

7 Mantras to Excel in Exams

—Prem P. Bhalla
Practical tips to score maximum marks

Exams play a major role in the lives of not just students, but adults too. Although youngsters are taught a variety of subjects to equip them for adult life, no school teaches them how to excel in exams. Most learn through trial and error. Others remain clueless about how to excel in exams throughout their lives. But this crucial information can ensure that even those with average IQ excel in exams. This book contains simple and practical tips and guidelines on how to tap your full potential and give off your best during exams. An invaluable guide for all students and adults preparing to appear in exams, as well as for parents who wish to ensure their children do well and secure maximum marks.

Simple guidelines on:
• Improving memory • Maximising concentration • Adopting effective study habits and techniques • Developing proper reading, listening, language, learning and communication skills • Doing well in different kinds of exams • Understanding what the examiner wants • Overcoming exam anxiety and tension

Demy Size • Pages: 144 (Also in Hindi)
Price: Rs. 80/- • Postage: Rs. 15/-